CW01456511

HOW TO BRING
UP A GENIUS?

© **2013 Michael Marcovici**

ISBN 9783735788832

„Herstellung und Verlag: BoD – Books on Demand, Norderstedt"

Bibliografische Information der Deutschen Nationalbibliothek: Die
Deutsche Nationalbibliothek verzeichnet diese Publikation in der
Deutschen Nationalbibliografie; detaillierte bibliografische Daten sind
im Internet über **www.dnb.de** abrufbar.

CONTENTS

HOW TO BRING UP A GENIUS

As many as 2% of children could potentially fall into the category of' gifted' so quite a few families can find themselves in the situation of having such a child to rear. This can raise a number of questions and issues to deal with – and they are not always positive.

Everyone likes to think their children are specially talented, above average intelligence, gifted in some respect. Often they might be right - but are they wishing something on themselves and the child that it is better not to have?

The history of child prodigies is mainly a story of difficulties, pressures, unfulfilled potential and often mental health and social problems that manifest themselves later in life. How the child develops might depend on the atmosphere and environment they are brought up in, the type of nurturing and encouragement they get and how their parents and institutions handle the stresses and challenges of dealing with what can often be a difficult young person.

Some child geniuses do grow up to be successful adults in useful occupations – though often they still fail in being rounded individuals. Others struggle with the expectations of being a prodigy or the social, emotional or personal pressures it brings and might drop out or end up working in McDonalds or in an office job (like Albert Einstein initially).

Many children identified as prodigies turn out to be very one-dimensional in their genius, perhaps having a flair for numbers or memorising lists, playing a musical instrument or learning languages, but lacking in other skills that make their talents useful or usable. There is a feeling that the standard education system fails these type of children. (There is probably a general feeling that education is letting most children down in our society today.)

This compilation looks at gifted children; what makes them gifted, how they can be nurtured and what eventually happens to them. It also recounts some specific histories of young genius and the problems and outcomes for some of the individuals endowed with these qualities.

We won't all have gifted children – and maybe that is not such a bad thing. Equally, if we, as parents, applied some of the nurture principles that are recommended for prodigies, perhaps the average child would benefit also and become a more successful, complete individual due to going through the process. The parents are, undoubtedly, important factors in the ultimate outcome. Perhaps some of the information here can help you determine what type of parent you would want to be in this context.

1

15 Signs You'll Raise a Genius

Anneli Rufus

Want a little Einstein around the house? There's no single best recipe, but studies prove that keeping TV out of the nursery, shelling out for music lessons, breastfeeding, having a big library, and withholding cookies are just a few ways to boost your child's chances of success.

What makes a genius? Even experts argue over whether IQ, EQ, executive function, and/or academic achievement matters most. Nature? Nurture? The role of genetics in intelligence—i.e., the extent to which our smarts are inherited—has long been an academic war zone. What can raise your child's chances? Cello lessons, French lessons, and juggling.

1. Thirty percent of children under the age of 2 have television sets in their bedrooms.

And 59 percent of under-2s watch two hours of TV every day. The American Academy of Pediatrics recently issued a warning urging parents not to let infants and toddlers watch TV. Giving tiny viewers no known benefits, TV impairs cognitive skills and wastes crucial brain-development time that should be spent conversing with real people, says infant-language expert Roberta Golinkoff, coauthor of Einstein Never Used Flashcards: How Our Children Really Learn—And Why They Need to Play More and Memorize Less. "Language is crucial to children's learning, and the language they get from the television is not tailored to their individual needs. It will not answer their questions or follow their leads, which is how you create smart kids."

Elizabeth A. Vandewater, et al. "Digital Childhood: Electronic Media and Technology Use Among Infants, Toddlers, and Preschoolers." Pediatrics, 119 (5), 1006-15.

2. Six-year-olds who were breastfed consistently as babies score 5 percent higher on IQ tests than their 6-year-old peers who were not.

This stat is based on a study that followed two groups of new Belarusian mothers and their children. One group of mothers breastfed their babies more exclusively (giving them no other food or liquid but breast milk) and for longer (up to a year) than the other group, which breastfed less exclusively and for shorter durations. The children in the first group scored higher in reading, writing, and mathematics. "The first thing a woman can do to raise a smart child is to breastfeed," says geneticist Ricki Lewis, author of The Forever Fix: Gene Therapy and the Boy Who Saved It. "Human milk has a greater percentage of fat than cow's milk, needed to insulate our abundant brain cells; a calf needs the protein in its milk for fast growth."

Michael S. Kramer, et al. "Breastfeeding and Child Cognitive Development."Archives of General Psychiatry, 65 (5), 578-584.

3. Children who play the piano or a stringed instrument score 15 percent higher on verbal skills than children who don't play an instrument.

The study that yielded this stat involved students from Boston-area music and public schools; their average age was 10, and the musicians among them had studied music for at least three years. As the authors point out, many previous studies show correlations between musical skills, language skills, and IQ. The question of causality remains: are smart kids good at music, and/or does music make you smart? "The idea that our genes control our fates is called genetic determinism," Lewis says. "We geneticists fight this idea all the time."

Marie Forgeard, et al. "Practicing a Musical Instrument in Childhood Is Associated with Enhanced Verbal Ability and Nonverbal Reasoning."

4. Children who are able to delay gratification 15 times as long as their more impatient peers score 210 points higher on their SATs.

In one famous study, children were told they could eat two cookies if they delayed eating the first one. Those who could wait 15 minutes before eating the first cookie scored 210 points higher on their SATs than those who couldn't wait more than one minute. Impulse control is a crucial factor in executive function. "Scientists know now that being a brainiac is not so much about IQ but about executive function," Golinkoff asserts. "The ability to switch between tasks, hold things in your working memory, and inhibit impulses is much more connected with success than IQ."

John Medina. Brain Rules for Baby: How to Raise a Smart and Happy Child from Zero to Five. Seattle: Pear Press, 2010.

5. A child who is raised in a home containing at least 500 books is 36 percent more likely to graduate from high school and 19 percent more likely to graduate from college than an otherwise similar child raised in a home containing few or no books.

Granted, this study was published in 2007, when books were still tangible objects. The gap widens exponentially when the children's parents are barely literate. "Success in school depends on more than just native intelligence. It also requires a good work ethic," says psychologist Eileen Kennedy-Moore, author of Smart Parenting for Smart Kids. "Children learn more from what we do than from what we say. Parents who love to read demonstrate to their children that reading is interesting, enjoyable, and worthwhile."

M.D.R. Evans, et al. "Family Scholarly Culture and Educational Success."Research in Social Stratification and Mobility, 28 (2), 171-197.

6. The children of women who used cocaine while pregnant are nearly five times as likely to be developmentally disabled as children in the general population.

Fourteen percent of children whose mothers used cocaine while pregnant have IQs below 70, according to a study published in the Journal of the American Medical Association. And 38 percent of children whose mothers used cocaine while pregnant are developmentally delayed. Want valedictorians? Crack is wack.

L.T. Singer, et al. "Cognitive and Motor Outcomes of Cocaine-Exposed Infants."Journal of the American Medical Association, 287, 1952-1960.

7. Overweight children score 11 percent lower on national reading tests than regular-weight children.

The Temple University scientists whose study includes this stat also found that overweight middle-schoolers had lower GPAs than their regular-weight peers, as well as worse school attendance, more detentions, and more tardiness. This study associates higher body mass with lower scholastic achievement. "Being sedentary has huge opportunity costs for children," Golinkoff says. "If they're watching TV or playing computer games, they're not interacting—and many of the things that make us 'smart' are things learned only in the nexus of social interaction."

Stuart Shore, et al. "Decreased Scholastic Achievement in Overweight Middle School Students." Obesity, 16 (7), 1535-1538.

8. Aerobic exercise increases children's executive functioning abilities by as much as 100 percent.

"The best results accrue, by the way, if you do the exercises with your children," writes molecular biologist John Medina in his book Brain Rules for Baby, which cites this statistic. "Encouraging an active lifestyle is one of the best gifts you can give your child. It may mean putting away World of Warcraft." In the same vein, Lewis advises parents: "Focus on what you can control: the environment ... There's a lot people can do to help their kids. It is what happens after you are born that's important, not what you inherit."

John Medina. Brain Rules for Baby: How to Raise a Smart and Happy Child from Zero to Five. Seattle: Pear Press, 2010.

9. People who attended preschool are 52 percent more likely to graduate from high school than people who didn't attend preschool.

The study that yielded this stat followed two groups of disadvantaged Michigan children from toddlerhood to age 40. One group attended a "high-quality" preschool program at ages 3 and 4; the other never attended preschool. By age 27, five times as many in the preschool group owned their own homes as those in the non-preschool group. By age 40, the non-preschoolers had been arrested on drug charges eight times as frequently as the preschool alumni, and twice as often for physical assault.

L. J. Schweinhart, et al. "Lifetime Effects: The HighScope Perry Preschool Study Through Age 40." Monographs of the HighScope Educational Research Foundation, 14.

10. Children born to 20-year-old fathers score 3 to 6 points higher on IQ tests than children born to fathers twice that old.

"Advanced paternal age is associated with an increased risk of neurodevelopmental disorders such as autism and schizophrenia, as well as with dyslexia and reduced intelligence," write the scholars whose study included this figure. "The offspring of older fathers show subtle impairments on tests of neurocognitive ability." The modern tendency to delay fatherhood might be cause for concern, the scholars suggest.

S. Saha, et al. "Advanced Paternal Age Is Associated With Impaired Neurocognitive Outcomes During Infancy and Childhood." PLoS Medicine, 6 (3).

11. Learning to juggle can increase the volume of gray matter in children's brains by 3 percent.

Brain structure is largely determined by genes, but not entirely. "Learning a difficult perceptual-motor skill—juggling— induced a 3 percent increase in the volume of gray matter in visual attention areas," write the Yale scholars whose report cites this figure. The volume of gray matter in the brain's frontal region is linked with general cognitive ability, the scholars avow.

Jeremy Gray and Paul Thompson. "Neurobiology of Intelligence: Science and Ethics." Nature Reviews Neuroscience, 5, 471-482.

12. Children in welfare-recipient families hear nearly four times fewer words per year than children in professional-class families.

The more words we hear, the bigger our vocabularies and the higher our academic achievement, according to the scholars whose research revealed that children in welfare families hear about 3 million words per year, while children in working-class families hear 6 million and children in professional-class families hear 11 million. (That boils down to 616 and 1,251 and 2,153 per day, respectively.) According to the study, welfare-recipient children know 500 words by age 3, compared with 750 and 1,100 in the other groups.

Todd R. Risley and Betty Hart. Meaningful Differences in the Everyday Experience of Young American Children. Baltimore: Brookes Publishing, 1995.

13. Kids who have studied a foreign language for two years have SAT scores 14 percent higher than those of kids who never studied foreign languages.

One year of foreign-language study was linked with slightly higher SAT scores, but two years yielded increases of 14 and

13 percent on the test's verbal and math portions, respectively, over the scores of students who had never studied foreign languages. Each additional year of foreign-language study yielded further increases. "The verbal scores of students who had taken four or five years of foreign language were higher than the verbal scores of students who had taken four or five years of any other subject," write the scholars whose research yielded this stat. Vive les conjugaisons.

Thomas C. Cooper. "Foreign-Language Study and SAT-Verbal Scores." Modern Language Journal, 71 (4), 381-387.

14. Students who spend more than two hours a day playing computer and video games score 9.4 percent lower on school exams than students who play no such games.

The effects of electronic game-playing on academic achievement spark intense debate. A study conducted on students in the U.K. compared the test results of frequent gamers with those of nongamers. "Not a single significant positive correlation was found between gaming frequency and academic performance," the researchers write. "Excessive videogame playing—like excessive anything—can interfere with schoolwork as well as reading for pleasure, playing outside, sleeping, or interacting directly with friends and families," says Kennedy-Moore.

Barry Ip, et al. "Gaming Frequency and Academic Performance." Australasian Journal of Educational Technology, 24 (4), 355-373.

15. The children of mothers who were exposed to pesticides while pregnant have 1.4 percent lower IQs per increment of exposure than children whose mothers were not exposed to pesticides.

Columbia University scientists studied 7-year-olds and their mothers, finding direct links between prenatal exposure to the common agricultural pesticide chlorpyrifos and lower IQs. The negative impact of pesticide exposure is even greater on working memory, one element of those crucial skills collectively called "executive function." The notion that invisible components of the air we breathe might lower our children's intelligence is daunting indeed.

V. Rauh, et al. "Seven-Year Neurodevelopmental Scores and Prenatal Exposure to Chlorpyrifos." Environmental Health Perspectives, 119 (8).

2

TELL-TALE SIGNS OF A GENIUS CHILD

Linda Serck

Another young child with an exceptionally high IQ has been accepted by Mensa.

Four-year-old Heidi Hankins from Winchester is said to have an IQ of 159 - just one point below that of Einstein and Stephen Hawking.

But what are the tell-tale signs for a parent that their child is gifted? Are the rows of sponge numbers they are setting out in actual fact a mathematical formula? Are they showing signs of musical talent while bashing on their glockenspiel? For some parents, experiencing unusual intelligence in their infant is a reality. In the case of Heidi, her parents noticed she was a bright child extremely early.

Her father, Matthew Hankins, said: "She started to try and talk from the minute she was born but obviously she couldn't verbalise anything.

"She would look you in the eye and attempt to speak. "When she could talk, before she was a year old, she was speaking in whole sentences." She was also quick to pick up reading skills.

"We put her on the laptop to watch CBeebies because we didn't have TV at the time," Mr Hankins said. "When we came back to her we found she was navigating around the website.

"First of all she was just clicking on the pictures that she liked but very quickly we realised she had taught herself to read the text and follow instructions.

"By the time she was two she could read primary school books."

She also taught herself to add and subtract.

Charles Dickens

With clever children it appears you cannot stop them from fast-tracking their learning.

British Mensa's gifted child consultant Lyn Kendall said she discovered her son Chris, who is now 30, as an infant teaching himself how to write before the rest of the household awoke.

Aged four, he would prefer to read Charles Dickens at school instead of playing He-Man with the other children in the playground.

Gifted children "often prefer the company of older children or adults," she said.

When Chris was invited to his classmates' parties "you could guarantee he'd be in the kitchen with a cup of tea chatting with the adults - and not racing round with the other kids".

So what other tell-tale signs are there that your child could be a genius?

Mensa has a checklist on its website that includes:

• An unusual memory

• Reading early

• Unusual hobbies or interests or an in-depth knowledge of certain subjects

Elise Tan Roberts from London was two when she joined Mensa in 2009 with a 156 IQ

• An awareness of world events

• Asks questions all the time

• Developed sense of humour

• Musical

• Likes to be in control

• Makes up additional rules for games

Educational psychologist

Mensa itself does not assess children below the age of 10, but if parents feel the need to have their child's IQ tested then they have to go through an educational psychologist.

As many of these do not assess children under six, having your infant tested can be costly - between £250 and £750, according to Julie Taplin, the deputy chief executive of the National Association of Gifted Children (NAGC).

Mr Hankins said the family wanted to get Heidi tested out of curiosity. He said: "Her brother was a bright child but this was kind of a league above, you know, supernaturally bright so we were just interested to see."

Ms Taplin said an assessment was not always necessary. "Some parents often think if they have a piece of paper that their child has a specific IQ that their school will therefore feel they must meet their child's needs and have the resources to do so," she said. "But schools are not obliged to look at the educational psychologist's report."

If parents do feel an IQ test is necessary, then the Weschler test is the one usually carried out on young children and is the test Heidi completed.

Oscar Wrigley from Reading was two when he scored an IQ of 160 in 2009

"It is a battery of tests," said Mrs Kendall, "looking at non-verbal functioning - your ability to solve a problem with things like shapes, looking at a verbal IQ - the use and understanding of language, numerical skills, problem solving and practical tests such as block formation."

Mrs Taplin said it was important to offer a support network for the child that focuses as much on their social and emotional skills as their schooling.

"Academic potential has to be balanced by the child's overall well-being," she said.

Parents also need to be aware of the some of the negative aspects of being a gifted child, including becoming aware of the world too quickly and not being able to interact with children of their own age.

Mrs Kendall said: "I will never forget when I first joined NAGC, one of the first young people I met said, 'I just want to be like everyone else - I hate being clever.'"

As for Heidi, Mr Hankins said she was interacting well at nursery. Next week the family will find out which primary school Heidi will be attending and she is extremely keen to join her friends who are already at school.

"We will need to sit down and talk to the school to see how we can keep her motivated because it will be extremely basic," said Mr Hankins. "They'll be teaching phonics and colouring in letters while she will be reading the Oxford Reading Tree books at level 6 and 7 for eight-year-olds.

"But we are fairly relaxed about it. She'll continue to do what she wants and she has done very well so far.

"We don't want to turn her off by pushing her."

http://www.bbc.co.uk/news/uk-england-hampshire-17702465

3

CHILD GENIUSES: WHAT HAPPENS WHEN THEY GROW UP?

Patrick Barkham

You're the girl with the sky-high IQ, the boy who's amazing at maths… and then what? Patrick Barkham quizzes bright sparks past and present

Karina Oakley, 3¾, has an IQ that is, at 160, the same as Stephen Hawking's

Karina Oakley: 'As soon as she started talking, it was like this massive word explosion.' Photograph: Graeme Robertson for the Guardian

"All of my horses are called Athena," announces Karina. Except for Sandy, that is, a small plastic creature with a wounded leg. Karina places Sandy in a bed she has made from Fuzzy Felt. "There you are, little horse. I'll give him some special horse medicine," she says. "Five lots of medicine. Now he's come back to play with his friends."

Karina is Charlotte Fraser's only child. They live, the two of them, with Truffles the cat, in Surrey. "As soon as she started talking, it was like this massive word explosion," Charlotte says. "Everybody she came into contact with would say, my goodness, how old is she?"

Charlotte thinks it is "a bit rotten" to compare Karina with friends' children"because they all develop in their own way and you don't want to be this competitive mum". But after a helper at the church creche noticed Karina's "incredible" imagination, Charlotte found a child psychologist on the internet and, a year ago, took her daughter to London for an IQ test. "Karina has an unusual air of maturity in one so young," said Professor Joan Freeman and, in a careful report pointing out the shortcomings of IQ tests in very young people, suggested that she had an IQ of 160 – said to be the same as Stephen Hawking's – which placed her in the top 0.03% of children of her age.

Asked in these tests what we do with our eyes, Karina said we put contact lenses in them. Shown a picture of a teapot without a handle and asked what was missing, she said the picnic mat.

Shown a picture of a glove that was lacking one finger and asked what was missing, she said the other glove.

Charlotte found it "reassuring" to discover that Karina was not suffering from some "really weird way of thinking". She does not know from where her linguistic precocity comes: Charlotte was adept at science, she says, and Karina's father, Nick (from whom Charlotte is separated), was good at physics and maths.

Stories of home-schooled geeks scare her. "What every parent wants for their children is to give them a happy, balanced, enjoyable childhood. I don't think any adult is ever going to go, 'Damn, I didn't do my GCSEs aged nine." So Karina goes to a local nursery and spends much of her time "junk modelling". She shows off a chocolate tray, decorated with tissue and paper: a butterfly feeding table.

While Charlotte has a few reservations about this "child-led" learning – "There's a bit of me that thinks it's a nursery, you're teachers, you could be doing something more with her" – she plans for Karina to attend her local primary school, along with her friends. "As she gets older, perhaps I will need to look at it again," Charlotte says. "I guess I worry if she gets bored at school. Sometimes it doesn't come out as 'bored' – it comes out as causing trouble at the back of the class."

Ishaan Yewale, 5, has memorised more than 600 London bus routes

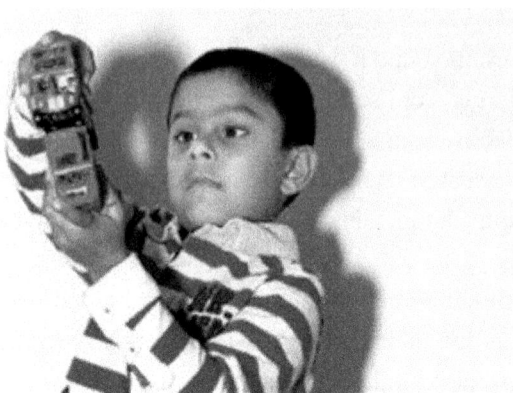

Ishaan Yewale: 'I can see buses from other buses.' Photograph: Graeme Robertson for the Guardian

How long have you been a bus fanatic? "The last five years," says Ishaan, sitting in front of a laptop looking at Transport for London bus maps.

Jay and Sonali Yewale moved to London from Mumbai 10 years ago for Sonali's job at Citigroup. Jay is a business development manager for an IT company. Just over six months ago, their only child, Ishaan, developed a thing for London buses and memorised more than 600 bus routes across the capital. It was not easy for him, Jay says, because, while Ishaan has a reading age of at least seven, there were some difficult location names to read. The memorising bit came easily.

So far, Ishaan's talent has taken him on to BBC Breakfast and ITV News, but he hasn't found the media coverage too demanding. Where did his interest come from? Does he see buses from their south London flat? "I can see buses from other buses," Ishaan trills in a singsong voice. "I can see DLR trains from there," he points to the front window. "And I can see National Rail from the kitchen." He runs into the kitchen to demonstrate.

Which are best, buses or trains? "Buses," Ishaan answers incisively. What is his favourite bus route? "The whole world," he says, somewhat tangentially. Later, he clarifies: his favourite route is actually the 108 from Lewisham to Stratford, which he travels on to school. How many buses does he see from his favourite bus? Roughly, I say. It's a stupid question and I am not expecting an answer. "I only saw 17 today," he says. "Ten when going and seven coming back."

Every few months, Ishaan finds a new obsession. Cricket was one – he learned to recognise virtually all the players in the IPL; Thomas the Tank Engine was another. His favourite engine is "Gordon, the biggest and the fastest. He goes at least 100mph. Other engines only go 50. And Thomas and Percy only go at 20. No, 25," he corrects himself.

His gentle parents seem rather bemused by their hyper-energetic little boy. He never wants to go to bed and has energy to burn at all hours. He is bilingual (he also speaks Marathi), and his school has run out of books for him. While his reading is good, he is among the worst at writing, Jay says. And if Ishaan doesn't like something, it's hard to get him to do it. Jay and Sonali were themselves both high achievers at Indian schools, which were far more competitive than British ones. "But I think he's ahead of us," Jay says.

They are keeping an eye on whether the school can meet his needs. So far, they say, they've been happy, but "it's early days", Jay says.

Megan Ward, 10, is an inventor; her anti-smoking keyring is already in production

Megan Ward: 'She thinks differently.' Photograph: Graeme Robertson for the Guardian

When Paula and Rory Ward are not running a plumbing and drainage company in Kent, they are busy marshalling the lives of their children, Alfie, six, Joe, eight, Charlie, 13, Steph, 19, and, squeezed in the middle, Megan, 10. While her home reverberates with footballing kids, sulky teens, three bounding dogs, a rabbit and a hamster called Spotty, Megan is quietly inventing. A year ago, she had to design an anti-smoking poster for a school project. Rather than a poster, she came up with the idea of creating a translucent, squidgy pair of lungs containing brown food colouring that shows the average amount of tar a smoker collects from just four packs of cigarettes.

"I like people to play with things more than read and write," she says. So she researched her idea on the internet, found a company in China that could make the device, saved up her pocket money and, with a bit of financial assistance from her mum, got her idea made. Paula helped her daughter get a patent and since then, anti-smoking consultancy Gasphas placed an order worth £12,000 for 25,000 of Megan's keyrings.

Megan is dyslexic. Paula says her daughter "thinks differently": she "prefers drawings and is obviously quite creative". Ideas pop into her mind when she watches TV. After she got sunburnt on holiday, Megan devised a small plastic bracelet that changes colour in the sun, telling you when to put on sunscreen, and a T-shirt that does the same thing. Several sunscreen companies have expressed an interest in the idea. "We were walking the dogs once and what did you come out with?" asks Paula. "A ball that could be filled with water and you called it Quetch – like fetch! – because it quenches a dog's thirst. But we didn't do anything with it. There's a lot we haven't done, but I backed her on the anti-smoking one because I thought, actually, Meg, it's good."

There is also Megan's idea for a dog collar containing a speaker so that owners can call their dog on the collar. Then she pulls out a picture of a special fishing rod she has designed. "There is a camera at the end of the rod, on the hook," she explains, "and it's waterproof, and the screen is on the handle, and it shows you if you've caught a fish or not."

Megan goes to Girl Guides, doesn't want to go to university, and likes the inventor Trevor Baylis, trampolining, the film Marley & Me, Miley Cyrusand The BFG. She keeps her pink-and-cream bedroom immaculately tidy. Paula is amazed and a bit confused by her daughter, who is a quiet, yet also slightly demanding presence in their hectic household. "Everything has to be routine," Paula says. "Her brothers and sisters go with the flow, but with Meg it's, 'What time will that be happening?' or, 'Where am I being picked up from today?' That's why, when she does enjoy something, I encourage her. She needs a lot of encouragement."

Niall Thompson, 16, started a maths degree at Cambridge aged 15

Niall Thompson: 'I think the media wish I was 4ft nothing with Harry Potter glasses and no friends and no personality.' Photograph: Graeme Robertson for the Guardian

"I was just normal in primary school," Niall Thompson says. Five years on, he started at Cambridge University aged just 15; the only child of a single mother from a family in which no one had ever gone to university.

His life changed in his first week at high school in Manchester. His maths teacher, Kate Parker, took him aside at the end of lessons and gave him an advanced textbook to try. He found it relatively easy, so Parker began teaching him after school, delaying her retirement by two years to help him. It was she who first suggested he try for Oxbridge. Classmates teased him, saying he and Parker were having a romance. "There were insinuations," he says. "I'd like to point out that she was 60."

After picking up an A* in his maths GCSE in Year 8, he took his A-levels in Year 10. His mum worried he worked too hard at school. Did he feel he was missing out on normal teenage life? "Not often," he says. He was relieved to leave Manchester for Cambridge. "It's good not to stick out for once."

Niall does not look any younger than many other boyish first-years at Cambridge. When he arrived he was nervous: "But two weeks later I was absolutely fine." He can call his personal tutor, Martin Hughes, any time on his mobile phone. Hughes, along with everyone in Niall's hall of residence, had a Criminal Records Bureau check.

Two terms in, Niall has not socialised much yet. He went out only once during freshers' week because everything was based around drinking. "That was the main difficulty," he says, "although that really doesn't bother me at all. Everyone should be working anyway."

He has not joined any clubs or societies ("I refused to join the Maths Society. If you're going to join a society, join a society that's different from what you'd be doing otherwise") and does not like sport, so instead he relaxes in his room. He is "never off Facebook", talking to Vicky, his best friend from home (although she's not in his good books right now after she posted on the internet some maths answers he gave her). He watches a lot of DVD boxsets – Shameless, Catherine Tate and, especially, Doctor Who. With his piercings and love of Paramore, he is a bit of an emo kid. "I'm not ashamed," he says.

Niall will graduate from university before his peers even start it. This kind of fast-tracking occurs nowadays only in maths, according to Hughes, where there is a belief that you peak early, burn out young, and if you haven't made your mark by 21, you never will. When Niall was little, he wanted to be a train driver and then a Concorde pilot. Now he does not know what he will do at 18; he thinks he may need a year out.

He found the media attention when he started at Cambridge a bit weird. "Sometimes I think they wish I was 4ft nothing with Harry Potter glassesand no friends and no personality," he says of journalists who meet him. Does he feel uncomfortable being called a child prodigy or a genius? "I've got used to it. I feel like I'm in my rightful place. I'm surrounded by people who think you're good if you're good at maths, and it's not considered strange."

Andrew Halliburton, 23, began studying maths with secondary school pupils at 8

Andrew Halliburton: 'I always felt I had to live up to that genius moniker, I never once thought I could.' Photograph: Graeme Robertson for the Guardian

Before Andrew was two, he recognised the numbers and letters when Countdown came on TV in the living room of the family's flat in Dundee. His dad, Al, a civilian police driver, and his mum, Jean, a cleaner, were baffled. "When he was young, I thought he was hyperactive," Jean says. "We had him at the doctors' and that's what they said. But he wasn't." Luckily, when Andrew was still very young, the council recognised his promise and provided him with a tutor and a computer.

Andrew did Mensa puzzles in newspapers and played on the computer in his bedroom. "I feel like my childhood was sort of wasted," he says. "I didn't really get to go out as much as other kids, but I did enjoy the typical stuff little boys did." Like riding bikes? He pauses. "I never did learn to ride a bike."

When he was eight, his primary school headteacher phoned around secondary schools to find somewhere he could study higher-level maths. At nine, his maths classmates were 13 and 14. "It didn't faze me," he says. He was big for his age, almost 6ft by the time he was 11, which was when he sat his standard level maths. For the first time in his life, he felt pressured and "started to panic". His peers, teachers and parents all expected him to do well. Then there was the media. A picture of him sitting on a pile of textbooks and holding up rulers hangs in his parents' living room. "Genius Andrew Halliburton" was how the Sun referred to him. But for a shy boy, talking to the media was tough. "I could hardly get my words straight," he says of a TV news appearance. "That built up a lot of pressure for me before the exam."

He ended up with a grade two. He took his highers more slowly, got top grades and went straight to an applied computing course at university. For years, this had been the ultimate goal. It was a disappointment. "I was pretty disheartened when I found out it was a lot easier than I'd expected," he says. "Uni was the one time I had a bit of trouble making friends, which was strange because I was with my own age group."

He dropped out in his first year and got a job at McDonald's. Out of place, and unsure of what to do with his life, he nearly got fired. "What could be worse than getting fired from McDonald's?" he says. Five years later, he is still there, a humble crew member who sometimes enjoys the surprised look on customers' faces when he does the sums in his head rather than going to the till. He's not bothered by the geek tag – "I always thought of myself as a bit of a nerd" – but balks at the word genius. "I never liked the term." Was it a burden? "Certainly. I always felt I had to live up to that genius moniker, I never once thought I could."

It shocks people, Andrew says, but he doesn't really like maths. He's going back to university in September, this time to pursue his real passion: computer game technology. "I always thought my parents wouldn't accept that," he says, but Al is "over the moon". "I was disappointed when he left university, but we didn't fall out. We expected a lot. We expected him to do well. I'm not saying he didn't live up to my expectations, because he went and got a job, but McDonald's is a bit of a dead-end job." Andrew looks at his mum and dad. "I feel I haven't lived up to my expectations," he says.

Jennifer Pike, 20, became, at 12, the youngest winner of Young Musician of the Year

Jennifer Pike: 'The number of young people I've met with somebody literally forcing them to do this...' Photograph: Graeme Robertson for the Guardian

Jennifer Pike is acutely aware that the number of musical prodigies whose early precocity has ended in tragedy could make up a full orchestra. And she knows of exceptionally talented contemporaries who have struggled with family expectations, and the machinations of the music business that burden a young soloist.

In 2002, Jennifer, aged 12, became the youngest winner of BBC Young Musician of the Year. Instead of burning out, she has taken what critics called "a slow-burn approach": she eschewed publicity for quiet but intense musical study, and is now balancing an undergraduate degree at Oxford with 40 concerts a year around the world.

We have long been fascinated by musical prodigies – Mozart famously began composing at five – but great artists are often seen as manipulated victims. "There are so many awful stories – Michael Rabinaccomplished everything by the time he was 20 and died tragically," Jennifer says. "It's an honour to be told you have a prodigious talent, but the word has unwanted associations, which is tough for a youngster."

We assume things come easily to gifted people. "I'm very serious and very dedicated," she says. "It is like a swan on water: there's a lot of paddling underneath." Her career has entailed sacrifices: her family did not go on holiday so she could play expensive, top-quality violins and there are many things, from basketball to skiing, she would like to do but can't, for fear of injuring her hands.

The daughter of Jeremy Pike, a talented composer who studied underHenryk Górecki in Poland and is head of composition at Chetham's School of Music in Manchester, Jennifer was taken to concerts as a baby. A few weeks before her fifth birthday, she picked up a violin. Her dad immediately spotted her natural talent; Jennifer says she just "hacked away enthusiastically".

Her drive, she says, was her own. "The number of young people I've met with somebody speaking for them, literally forcing them to do this... I am lucky. I have a very inspiring and supportive family." As a child, she always wanted to do more practice and play more; it was she who had to push her teachers. "It's funny, the mentality of England is often, 'Let's just keep everybody at the same level', rather than assisting individual needs."

She went to Chetham's aged eight, then, at 16 and with one A-level in music to her name, was taken on by the Guildhall School of Music & Drama to do a three-year postgraduate course in music. Last autumn, she started an undergraduate music degree at Oxford. "I am really going for the whole life of being a student, not only to broaden those musical horizons, but really engage with young people. That will enrich my concert experience." To be a concert violinist, she believes you have to experience "normal" ("I hate using that word") life. When not practising, she watches old films and listens to jazz, Snow Patrol, Coldplay and even heavy metal on her iPod. "You have to be a really grounded person to communicate music."

She doesn't feel gifted. "I feel lucky to have this passion for music. It is just like speaking, in a way; what you say is completely spontaneous and you don't know what is making you say these things."

John Nunn, 54, was, at 15, the youngest Oxford undergraduate since Cardinal Wolsey

John Nunn: 'I don't like this child prodigy/genius thing. Human abilities are multifaceted.' Photograph: Graeme Robertson for the Guardian

In 1970, when John Nunn was 15, excited newspapers reported he'd become probably the youngest Oxford undergraduate since Cardinal Wolsey in the 15th century. Unlike many celebrated underage undergraduates who followed, John didn't go off the rails. He obtained his degree, taught at Oxford and became a professional chess player, rising to grandmaster and winning tournaments. He is now a successful chess author and publisher, living in Surrey with his wife, son and at least 1,200 books about chess with exotic, sinister titles: Mastering The Najdorf, Beating The Sicilian II.

John's father noticed he was unusual when, at three, he memorised the number of pages of every book in the bookcase. At four, he was taught to play chess by his father and, at seven, began beating him. He won his first championship aged nine and at 10 went to the comprehensive near his home in Roehampton, south-west London, a year early. He took maths O-level at 12, two maths A-levels at 14.

Taking classes with children four years older did not bother him: "I was too young to have social anxiety. I just got on with it." He remembers "a relatively normal childhood" kicking about Putney Heath. Unlike other extremely bright children, he never attracted derogatory nicknames and never became disruptive. "The chess helped. It was something else I could turn my mind to."

At Oxford, things got trickier: "Most of the boys were a few years older than me and into girls and drinking and things." In those days, there were no CRB checks or special help for a 15-year-old undergraduate: he shared a room with a "nice" 18-year-old geologist who proved useful when John needed help shooing nosy reporters off the premises. "I'm not sure he had his geologist's hammer with him when he went out," he laughs.

The labels that go with early achievement irritate him. "I don't like this child prodigy/genius thing. OK, you're a bit ahead of other people in one particular subject, but there is just this spectrum. Human abilities are multifaceted."

John detects a profound difference between modern childhood and his youth. As a child, he would play in the garden, read, do a bit of maths or chess. "With all the conflicting claims on children's time now, it's easy not to develop a particular talent which you might have done if you devoted more time to it."

4

THE LEGEND OF THE DULL-WITTED CHILD WHO GREW UP TO BE A GENIUS

Barbara Wolff & Hananya Goodman

At the age of 26, the patent clerk Albert Einstein emerged with a couple of scientific papers that soon would be considered products of an extraordinary creative mind.

How does that match the image of the young Albert labeled dull, dyslexic, even autistic or schizophrenic, by a considerable number of today's experts and interested parties?

In order to find a reliable answer, we should abstain from repeating, and perpetuating, all the dubious conjectures spread decades after Einstein's death, and rely, first of all, on the contemporaneous, original sources to determine whether any of these labels actually apply to the real Einstein.

In that context, a widely held belief regarding Einstein's handedness can immediately be rebutted. As photos show him holding a pen in his right hand, seizing a paper with the right hand and playing the violin like a right-hander, and as no evidence was found of him being or originally having been left-handed, one may take for granted that he was a right-hander. All this being said, little, though, is known about Albert Einstein's early years.

In the recollections of the family recorded by Einstein's younger sister, Maja, in 1924, Albert appears as a calm, dreamy, slow, but self-assured and determined child. Another three decades later, Einstein himself told his biographer, Carl Seelig, that "my parents were worried because I started to talk comparatively late, and they consulted a doctor because of it."

The grandparents, visiting two-year-old Albert, did not observe any developmental particularities and, in a letter to other family members, expressed enthusiasm about the grandson's good behavior and "drollige Einfälle" (funny or droll ideas or vagaries). Yet the reputed handicap of late talking became part of the family legend and is confirmed by Maja. The same family legend, though, reports that, at the age of 2 ½ years, when his newborn sister (a Mädle) was shown to the boy, Albert, obviously expecting a toy to play with, could already verbalize his disappointment: "But where are its wheels (Rädle)?" Might one assume that the "comparatively late" talking reflects the anxiety of an overambitious mother rather than the child actually having an identifiable problem?

As a matter of fact, the boy was, and remained, a reluctant talker for quite some years, and, until the age of about seven, used to repeat his sentences to himself softly, a habit which contributed to the impression he might be somewhat dull.

After one year of homeschooling, Albert was sent to primary school, entering second grade already at age 6 ½. He may not easily have accommodated himself to the school's expected mindless obedience and discipline aimed at instilling authoritarian civic virtues. Unable – or unwilling - to provide quick automatic responses, the boy was considered only moderately talented by his teachers. Yet at the end of his first school year his mother could proudly relate that Albert's report card was splendid and his second term marks again put him at the top of his class. If the stigma of the "bright under-achiever" - "The Einstein Factor" - had been justified at any time, now it was no more the case. The fact that, at the age of 9 ½, Albert was accepted to the competitive Luitpold-Gymnasium, disproves any observable learning disabilities. Had his grades in primary school not been above average, his entrance into the Gymnasium would not have been possible.

While the social milieu of his Gymnasium class, as well as the subject matter, were significantly more sophisticated and challenging than at the primary school, the teaching style continued to resemble the style Albert had despised already during his first school years. Learning facts and texts by rote was highly prized, while independent and creative thinking was perceived as undermining the teacher's respect. As it is the case with most pupils, Albert did not take the same interest in all subjects, but did advance well in general; in particular he advanced in subjects he favored even doing so far beyond his age.

In his later years, Einstein repeatedly pointed out that memorizing words, texts, and names caused him considerable difficulties. Yet, if one regards the pupil's alleged "learning disability" in the context of his distaste for the teaching style which he experienced as military drill, and of his own mental preoccupations, then a psychological block seems a much more plausible explanation than medical "dyslexia". Moreover, not only did Albert advance from grade to grade without having to repeat a grade, even in the subject of Greek – with which an unsympathetic teacher predicted that he would never get anywhere - Albert received final marks of 2 out of 4, with 1 as the highest mark.

But, yes, he flunked the entrance exam at the Zurich Polytechnic. Albert left his Munich Gymnasium in the middle of the seventh of nine obligatory high-school years, at the age of 15. When, with special permission, he presented himself for the entrance exam at the Zurich Polytechnic in the following autumn, he was still one and a half years short of the required age to enter that college. Also, as German and Swiss school curricula differ substantially, his knowledge, for instance, of French and of some general subjects definitely did not meet Swiss high-school diploma standards. So it was the circumstances that 'handicapped' Einstein, rather than his own personal inabilities. More noteworthy than the fact that he failed the exam is that his knowledge in mathematics and physics impressed his examiner in such a way that he invited the boy to his college lectures even before Albert was accepted as a regular student.

To provide evidence of a "learning disability" it has been argued that Einstein's special talents in particular subjects were linked to an exceptionally strong deficiency in other areas. Einstein's own words, too, appear to substantiate his impediment in languages, and as early, seemingly impartial evidence of his weakness in languages the above-cited exam is often mentioned. An attempt to learn Hebrew, Einstein is quoted in 1923 as saying, would be unproductive work for him. And from numerous reports of his American years we know that until the end of his life German was the only language he felt comfortable with.

But in the entrance exam to the Polytechnic, that he took after only half a year of French lessons at the Gymnasium, Albert had to compete with Swiss graduates who had at least six years of French study. And the statement with respect to the Hebrew language was the realistic evaluation of a 43-year-old scientist who had no use for that particular language and, therefore, no motivation to learn it. Ten years later, the American immigrant was well able to acquire the necessary knowledge to communicate with his new compatriots. Would anyone be surprised that at the age of fifty-five he did not reach the same high level in English as he did in his mother tongue, and had, another decade later, to admit that he "cannot write in English, because of the treacherous spelling?"

If dyslexia is defined as a neurological condition which causes problems translating language to thought or thought to language and therefore presents difficulties with reading, writing and spelling, speaking or listening, Einstein can certainly not be diagnosed with this defect.

The strongest argument that Einstein was not dyslexic is that he mastered the German language perfectly and his ability to express himself in writing and speech showed high skills of comprehension, discrimination and precision.

A different aspect may be Einstein's social behavior. It prompted some specialists to place him among those afflicted with autism, or its milder form, a developmental disorder called Asperger's Syndrome. Children suffering from AS are characterized as aloof and emotionally detached; their socially inappropriate behavior and their extreme egocentricity prevent them from interacting successfully with their peers. They appear to have little empathy for others and to lack social or emotional reciprocity. Other symptoms include motor clumsiness, non-verbal communication problems, repetitive routines and stereotyped mannerisms and the idiosyncrasy for loud or sudden noises. One of the most interesting aspects of their personality is the "perseveration," an obsessive interest in a single object or topic to the exclusion of any other.

Some of the characterizations of AS described in the paragraph above actually apply well to the young Albert as we know him from Maja's and Max Talmey's recollections.

Both Maja and Talmey describe a boy who took little interest in boisterous games and, in general, in his peers, a boy who would concentrate patiently on elaborate constructions with building blocks or playing cards, delve into books and tricky arithmetic problems or play the violin. A sort of glass pane, as he called it many years later, separated him from his fellow human beings. Had such "social phobia" then been classified as a personality disorder, and had his parents and doctors felt the need to 'heal' the boy by making him conform to some norm, Albert might not have become Einstein.

Self-sufficiency, autonomy, a certain shyness and an extraordinary power of concentration, are traits that still characterized the adult scientist. He never felt comfortable with the obligation to deliver addresses and speeches and to mingle with people. The man who attracted women "like a magnet attracts filings", who was not afraid of having more than one love affair alongside his marriage and who stuck by his friends and lovers "in his way", this man nevertheless considered himself a lone wolf: "I never belonged to my country, my home, my friends, or even my immediate family, with my whole heart." Music was the portal into the place where Einstein sealed his emotions in order to avoid dealing with interpersonal relationships.

Although he did not expressly refer to himself when once he suggested that young scientists assume the function, for instance, of a lighthouse guard, we know from many similar statements that the adult Einstein relished solitude, be it in his study, be it on a sailing boat or elsewhere.

Yet, he had adjusted himself, to a certain degree, to the requirements of society. It is this "certain degree" that today's experts are focussing on. While the mature Einstein was obviously a high-functioning member of his society, he nevertheless displayed some peculiarities that did not really fit in. Such peculiarities, however, were tolerated by his fellow men, even considered irrelevant, and not abnormal, thus not pathological, thus not in need of a cure. His temporary states of absent-mindedness and forgetfulness were amusedly looked at as the flip-side of his concentration on problems with which he was preoccupied. No one would have insinuated that forgetting his keys or not remembering the names of persons with whom he had little connection, constituted symptoms of a disease.

His autonomy, fostered by his mother from an early age, was considered paradoxically both as a sign of maturity and as the fortunate retention of childlike curiosity and playfulness. Since such independence obviously constituted one of the prerequisites of his exceptional creativity, its unconventional or inconvenient aspects served as a target only for those who pursued political aims. These advocates of a different political philosophy, fascists and partisans of "German Physics" would have been jubilant to learn from today's experts that the creation of the theory of relativity could have only come from a schizophrenic mind capable of viewing things from the outside.

The boundary between socially tolerated "deviant" behavior on the one hand and pathological conduct on the other hand is re-defined by each society and in each era. Behavioral disorders exist only in relation to a concrete historical situation; developmental anomalies are deviations from a norm set at a given time by a distinct social group. Moreover, the same evidence can be construed in very different ways by different experts.

Einstein was no doubt an exceptional person. He was highly gifted and acquired early in his life the ability to exploit his talents. The stimulating milieu of his childhood, an ambitious mother who supported the son's self-reliance, and a counterbalancing and comforting father provided the environment where the child could develop his own personality. The "Creator and Rebel" eventually found a way of reaching self-actualization in the framework of his society.

Who dares to determine ex post facto, whether Einstein's genius is a result of autistic traits or of schizophrenic features? As long as the experts base their judgments on outright erroneous assertions about his childhood deficiencies, on misunderstandings regarding his performance at school, or on trivia of the kind of "He let his hair grow long and did not comb it. He wore old clothes and did not care about style", those judgments can hardly pass for reliable scientific expertise. As long as the same symptom is cited as an evidence of schizoid traits by one and as proof of being an autism spectrum disorder by another expert, one ought rather trust a third expert who frankly admits that while a pre-mortem diagnosis of a disorder with no known biologic markers would seem difficult enough, definitive post-mortem diagnoses are clearly impossible.

http://www.albert-einstein.org/article_handicap.html

5

THE GENIUS OF MOZART

Aaron Green

A Classical Music Child Prodigy

Wolfgang Amadeus Mozart

As I mentioned in the Mozart Profile, Mozart was born to a musical family. His father was a talented violinist and composer who regularly performed in churches and noble courts. He also wrote a well-known book called, A Treatise on the Fundamental Principles of Violin Playing. Mozart's older sister also played the keyboard, and together, they would travel the country to perform.

Mozart: The Child Prodigy

Mozart began showing his talents when he was just three years old. Thanks to the annotations made by his father in his sister's keyboard lessons book, we learned when and how long it took Mozart to learn the same music his sister was playing. It became clear that Mozart rapidly advanced through his sister's lesson book. Mozart's father began touring Mozart and his sister not just locally, but also internationally! During their trip to London , Mozart's abilities were tested "scientifically." In a famous report written by Daines Barrington, we learn about Mozart's extraordinary talents. Barrington brought a manuscript, never before seen by Mozart, which was composed with 5 parts with one part written in an Italian style Contralto clef, and set it in front of the young Mozart, just 8 years old, sitting at the keyboard. Barrington writes:

The score was no sooner put upon his desk, than he began to play the symphony in a most masterly manner, as well as in the time and stile which corresponded with the intention of the composer...

Impressed by Mozart's performance, Barrington requested to Mozart to improvise and perform a Love Song in operatic style that Barrington's famous opera singer friend, Manzoli, would choose to perform. Barrington again writes:

[Mozart] began five or six lines of a jargon recitative proper to introduce a love song. He then played a symphony... It had a first and second part, which together with the symphonies, was of the length that opera songs generally last: if this extemporary

composition was not amazingly capital, yet it was really above mediocrity, and shewed most extraordinary readiness of invention.

Again, an impressed Barrington made a similar request to Mozart, only this time to perform a *Song of Rage.* Mozart, again, presented a similar performance, except he *"beat his harpsichord like a person possessed, rising sometimes in his chair."* Afterward, Barrington had Mozart complete a series of difficult keyboard lessons. Barrington once again writes of Mozart:

His astonishing readiness, however, did not arise merely from great practice; he had a thorough knowledge of the fundamental principles of composition, as, upon producing a treble, he immediately wrote a base under it, which, when tried, had very good effect. He was also a great master of modulation, and his transitions from one key to another were excessively natural and judicious...

Barrington also noted that Mozart spent a great amount of time practising the harpsichord with the keys covered by a handkerchief.

http://classicalmusic.about.com/od/biographies/a/mozart-child-prodigy.htm

6

Uncovering the Truth of Mozart

Michael DeJager

Introduction

From Galileo to Einstein, mankind is familiar with the famous child prodigies who grew into the movers and shakers in their respective fields. Radically changing and developing fields of science, art, and music, prodigies have shaped the backbone of modern culture. Wolfgang Amadeus Mozart was undoubtedly one of the geniuses who revolutionized the world of music in the eighteenth century. Though relatively unappreciated for much of his life, his influence was hardly contained in his hometown of Salzburg or the city of Vienna after his death. Without his nonpareil perspective and prodigious compositions, much of modern classical music would not have developed in its current form.

Despite the respect that Mozart has received for his commitment to the creation of music, there are many misconceptions surrounding Mozart and his life. Tainted perceptions of

Mozart through films such as Amadeus and misconceptions in prodigy stereotypes have caused Western culture to develop a somewhat incorrect perception of Wolfgang Amadeus Mozart. Playing piano by three, writing symphonies by eight, and composing his first opera at the age of twelve, Mozart embodies the true image of a child prodigy (Kehoe).

Uncovering the true Wolfgang Amadeus Mozart is a tall order. Mozart's upbringing and background assist in explaining why he had problems later in life. The idea of a "prodigy" is very vague, and it is significant to further explore the causes and perceptions of prodigies in the eighteenth century in comparison to the present. Furthermore, Mozart viewed himself through eyes of disdain. How can a prodigy expect to be successful when he is combating low self-esteem? Finally, how has Mozart played a role in impacting today's culture, continuing to live on through his music almost three hundred years after?

Mozart as a Prodigy

A prodigy is one who is endowed with special or exceptional qualities, particularly in a given field. Mozart easily falls in the category of a prodigy because of his natural abilities in the field of music. "In a sense, Mozart defines what it means to be a prodigy: Astounding talent, astonishingly early productivity at the highest levels, and a powerful personality seem to capture the essence of the prodigy" (Feldman). Prodigies can be found in every field as those who naturally have a knack for something. Understanding the characteristics of prodigies is crucial when discussing Mozart. According to David Henry

Feldman, there are ten commonalities among prodigies. While not all of these may apply to every prodigy, these are good indicators to examine.

Family history plays a major role in the development of a prodigy. Generally speaking, prodigies emerge from families with a family history of interest in the special field of the prodigy. It isn't likely that an amazing artist is going to suddenly spring out of a family that has had generational scientists over the past two centuries. Mozart follows this rule to some extent because the musical genes do not root deep within his lineage. Leopold had the aspiration of becoming a court musician and, therefore became fairly adept in the musical world; however, a couple of other relatives exhibited interest in music.

For some reason, prodigies tend to appear as the first-born in a family. They also tend to be of the male gender. Mozart was technically not the first-born male of the family. He was the first and only surviving male of his family. As Nannerel was four years older than Mozart, he was exposed to music as she was starting to learn. By the time Mozart was four, Leopold knew that Wolfgang had a real talent for music because of his interest in Nannerel's lessons.

Next, prodigies are not gifted in everything. Prodigies are exceptionally talented in very certain and specific areas. This does not mean that they don't do well in other fields. It just means that they are not exceptional in all areas. Though Mozart was good at math and proficient in multiple languages, his abilities in those areas reflected an extremely developed mind. Those abilities nowhere compared to his abilities in music.

Sufficient resources must be present in order for a potential prodigy to take root and flourish as a child. Resources do not necessarily imply monetary support; however, it may be necessary depending on the situation. In Mozart's case, Leopold was able to facilitate an outstanding environment because of his intense schooling. Mozart never attended school, but it wasn't necessary as his father taught him everything from a variety of languages to how to play different instruments. As the focal point of a strong support system, as well as a complete musical tour of Europe at a young age with Nannerel and his family, Mozart was provided with the resources for success.

For prodigies, it takes approximately ten years, sometimes more, to develop their talent completely. If the sufficient resources do not exist to sustain this development, it is likely that prodigies will never reach their full potential. In regard to Mozart, he started his musical career at the very young age of three. By age thirteen, his abilities were almost fully developed; however, it still took most of his teenage years to develop the style and sound that he became famous for and is still known for today.

Another significant quality typical of prodigies is single-mindedness. Single-mindedness pertains to one's ability to stay focused on one thing and be driven to become the best at it. This was very much a part of Mozart's outlook; however, he also balanced this with a strong desire for social connections. Even though he was home-schooled, he had the opportunity as a child to travel, showing off his natural ability. This not only helped grow the prodigy within, but it also instilled him with a strong social desire. Confidence in oneself is a significant trait of a prodigy. Mozart understood his abilities early on, even possessing the ability to assess the compositions of other composers of the time. He never appeared to doubt his ability to perform and compose.

Another commonality among prodigies is something equivalent of a "midlife crisis" sometime during adolescence. They may begin to question their abilities or to have concerns facing the adult world. As a prodigy's mind develops so quickly, it would make sense to a have a major crisis at such an early age. For Mozart, this took the form of a love relationship. He fell hopelessly in love with a young singer and wanted to pursue his relationship with her instead of pursuing his own musical career. As his father controlled him, there was no hope for Mozart to gain his father's support of relationships in his life.

Prodigies often provoke hostility and ambivalence from those with whom they interact. Usually from competitors, prodigies will face jealousy or other forms of malice toward their outstanding abilities. Mozart brought more disbelief and awe to the table than anything else, accompanied with a lot of positive reactions and genuine recognition for his abilities. The idea of a prodigy was not even looked upon as favorable during Mozart's time. Prodigies were considered deviant entities and unique anomalies to the norms. As a result of this, Mozart was more referred to as a miracle of his time.

Finally, because of the environment necessary in order to foster the development of a prodigy, they usually exhibit some adult and some childlike characteristics. All focus is put on the development of the skill in which prodigies exhibit natural talent. Because of this, other basic skills learned as a child are often thrown by the wayside such as tying your shoes or cooking a meal. For Mozart, childlike qualities were imbedded in his compositions throughout his life. This unique quality is one element that set his music apart from others at the time. His scatological humor, something he never grew out of, also exhibited immaturity.

Besides Feldman's interpretation of prodigious qualities, other theories have been set forth to explain the development of prodigies. William Therivel explains the GAM theory of personality. "G stands for genetic endowment, A for assistances of youth, M for misfortunes of youth." These traits give rise to a challenged personality, therefore, having the ability to sustain high levels of creativity. "Challenged personalities have a superior potential for creativity because (a) lacking many of the common scripts, they develop many of their own scripts which constructively clash with the common scripts of society, and (b) they possess a powerful drive to accomplish" (Therivel).

Mozart was endowed, for whatever reason, with an uncanny musical ability. From playing different instruments to composing music, Mozart was a natural. Next, Mozart was provided all of the assistance he needed through his main significant other: his father. As Leopold was everything from Mozart's teacher to his business manager throughout all of his younger years, Mozart was provided with the environment to flourish as a young musician. Finally, "Mozart's major misfortune of youth was that of paternal failure of character and profession. This is one of the most challenging misfortunes when compensated by quality assistances" (Therival).

Prodigies are a phenomenon in society. It should be noted that the role of a mentor as well as a proper environment in which to flourish is understated. There are undoubtedly many more potential prodigies in the world who have never emerged due to the lack of a significant other in their life.

http://www.jwu.edu/uploadedFiles/Documents/Academics/ JWUHonPaperMozartDNV.pdf

7

GENIUS: THE NEUROBIOLOGY OF GIFTEDNESS

Irma Iskandar

Toby Rosenberg, in all the five years of his life, has never been your typical toddler. At age 14 months, Toby could read aloud from posters his stroller passed by. A year later, he spoke both Polish and English fluently, and at the age of 4, he compiled a dictionary of hieroglyphics after visiting a museum shop and perusing through a book on ancient Egypt. From W.A. Mozart to Bobby Fisher to Toby Rosenberg, some children have since their birth amazed the world with their incredible intellect and abilities that can at times outdo even the brightest of adults. Why is this so, and, as many parents-to-be wonder, can a genius be created? It is evident that when a child's mental development is displayed far beyond the usual time, the only reasonable explanation is that the brain and nervous system are much more highly developed than is normal for the age. Some scientists believe that there are quantitative differences in these children's cerebral organization, and that these differences may possibly have a genetic link. However, although results seem to indicate this as so, more data is needed to establish this firmly and to ultimately explain why so few children have such gifted abilities.

First, however, one must have a clear notion of what is meant by giftedness. Only the top 2-5 % of children in the world are truly gifted. These children are precocious, self-instructing, can intuit solutions without resorting to logical, linear steps, and have an incredible interest in an area or more that they focus so intently on, that they may lose sense of the outside world. Early reading and development of abstract thought are typical characteristics as well. The acceleration of mental growth, however, is not the only factor involved in giftedness. The final stage of development is formal operative thinking, which is the ability to move beyond the concrete world and work with abstractions. Although until recently scientists had believed that these are stages normal in adults, studies now indicate that many college freshmen and even adults have not yet reached this stage. Having such advanced cognitive abilities and early development, therefore, appears to be characteristics of the gifted. Why do such few children have these characteristics? The answer remains unsolved; however, neurological studies seem to hint towards several answers.

The study of the gifted brain has been utilized by scientists throughout much of history. The effort to reduce genius to bulges in the brain has its roots in 19-th century pseudoscience, where phrenologists pinned personality traits to swatches of the cortex and measured the size of bumps on people's heads. Vain Victorian intellectuals bequeathed their brains to craniometers, in order to measure up to the myth "bigger is better". Today, various neuroimaging, more reliable technologies have been used to determine differences in brain structure between the gifted and those of average intelligence. The gifted brain is implicated in having more numerous, more complex, and more active neural connections. PET and EEG tests have revealed that the brain organization of exceptionally mathematically-inclined teenagers are atypical to some extent - several areas of the cortex are more differentiated in the gifted teenager's brain, especially the frontal areas, than those of his or her peers. In another EEG study where the alpha wave power of mathematically-gifted teenagers were compared to that of SAT-matched college students, results showed that the gifted students had superior alpha wave power, and superior frontal activity. The hippocampus of the gifted, a major area involved in memory, was found to be not as compartmentalized as those of lower achieving students. In another study, the examination of Albert Einstein's brain yielded findings of a larger-than-normal, un-folded parietal lobe, an area of the brain that is usually folded and that is associated with visuo-spatial and mathematical abilities. Although many tests have been undertaken with various results, one may fathom that many factors may be influenced in the brain of a genius, and that no one area of the brain may be responsible for giftedness. Furthermore, the prospect of external environmental factors in influencing the development of the brain has not even been discussed in this paper, although some scientists believe that these factors are extremely influential. It is easy, therefore, to see how complex finding the answer to giftedness may actually be.

Furthermore, neurophysiologists have disputed whether genius can be mainly localized in the right hemisphere of the brain or not. For example, Alexander, O'Boyle, & Bendow (1996) have suggested that "enhanced right-hemisphere involvement occurring during information processing, as well as superior coordination and allocation of cortical resources within and between the hemispheres, are unique characteristics of the gifted brain." In another study, average students tested on verbal skills thought in the left hemisphere only: however, when mathematically talented children were tested, both the left and right hemispheres were implicated in controlling language - therefore, the right side was participating in tasks originally reserved for the left. Although findings about left and right hemisphericity may hint towards generalizations regarding their role in mental activity, one must keep in mind that many exceptions were found that defy association with particular locations of the brain.

As this paper has suggested, although various answers regarding areas in the brain have been implicated in localizing genius, no strong conclusion may follow, except the fact that many areas of the brain may be involved in the process. There are also disadvantages with the technologies used in making these findings- for example, PET is not suitable to use for young children (the age-group needed most for these findings) and is temporally insensitive. EEGs may have weak signals that are corrupted by the thickness of the skull, and is spatially insensitive to the mid-brain. Furthermore, although physical parts of the brain may be implicated, what can one suggest about other factors such as genes and the external environment? How could one make sure that Einstein's genius wasn't due to enlarged parietal lobes but childhood experiences, his readings (he had owed his theory of relativity to his reading of David Hume's A Treatise of Human Nature, or a million other factors? Other insights I found that could be derived from the study of giftedness is that we still do not know what makes one smarter than another - smart parents have children of average intelligence, intellectually challenged parents have brilliant children. Genius children have thrived in areas where the environment is not conducive to learning, and may have superior reading skills for their age despite there being very few books in the house. Although parents eager to make their kids super-geniuses may put them in a constant intellectually stimulating environment, still only 2-5% of the population of children are considered truly gifted.

In conclusion, more data is needed to establish firmly the significance of brain differences in gifted and average children, and to ultimately explain why so few children have such gifted abilities. There are many facets about the brain that are still indeterminate - however, a stronger realization is that regarding even the most desirable traits, being a genius may to a large extent be beyond a person's control, and cannot be intentionally created. Sometimes, no matter how ambitious a person may be or how mentally stimulating an environment may be, the desired results are not fulfilled. This lack of knowledge about genius is a present problem - in the future, however, perhaps scientists will find what exactly makes a person brilliant. Genetic engineering could be utilized to artificially induce areas of the brain to be larger than normal, or less compartmentalized in terms of memory. Having a genius child could be as simple as paying a visit to a doctor's office. Perhaps then it is best not to know what makes a genius child tick. In this way, humans can avoid the mundane prospect of reducing human intelligence to scientific measurements of brain features with the use of a brain scan.

http://serendip.brynmawr.edu/bb/neuro/neuro01/web2/
Iskander.html

8

How to Raise a Genius

Nicholas Weinstock

Last summer, after much consideration, Toby Rosenberg
announced to his friends and family that he had decided to
change his name. "Toby," he felt, was "a little boy's name."
Going forward, he would be called Karl, like his father before
him. His school made note of the switch. His parents had no
argument. Toby -- now Karl -- was 5 years old.

And he had a point: regardless of his age, Karl has never been a
little boy. At 14 months, he began to read aloud from the posters
he was pushed past in his stroller. It would be another full year
before he truly conversed; but once he did, his fluent English
and Polish (his mother, Anna, 40, is from Krakow) were soon
joined by other languages. He trained himself to write Japanese
after studying the side of a sake bottle. He taught himself the
Hebrew alphabet after catching sight of the characters on a
dreidel. Last year, after seeing a book in a museum shop on
ancient Egypt, he compiled a dictionary of heiro-glyphics. The

impression you get upon making his acquaintance is that of a bookish teenager, a middle-aged Polish diplomat and a gabby Brooklyn grandmother trapped together in the taut body of a first grader.

"You don't know what it's like with Karl," his father says, laughing tiredly. An artist turned Web-site designer, Karl Sr., 61, spends at least an hour every afternoon in the family's one-bedroom Brooklyn apartment drafting sketches and submitting them to his son's critiques. "He stands behind me and tells me to draw things over and over to his specifications," Karl says. "Beam construction, Russian churches. If he's not on the Internet, he's here, issuing commands over my shoulder. We just want to encourage his interests and support him any way we can. Nobody in this household is trying to tell him what to do." Which is just as it should be.

1. Don't overstructure your child's life. Experts advise parents of hyper-intelligent children not to be too controlling. "Profoundly gifted kids are highly curious and likely to pursue all kinds of interests with great passion," says Sandra Berger, a gifted-education specialist for more than 20 years. "It's best to let the child's interests be your guide, and to follow the path created by his or her love of learning. As a parent, if you try and put yourself in that path, you're likely to get knocked around."

2. Provide as many learning opportunities as possible. Parents should strive to introduce their children to as wide an array of subjects as they can, not only through field trips and museum tours but also by treating everyday surroundings as experiential playgrounds. It was reportedly his early rambles in the woods with his father that alerted Richard Feynman, the Nobel-prize-winning physicist, to the complexity of life. For Karl, it was drives past the Williamsburg Bridge that piqued his avid interest in truss construction.

Such interests can prove a distraction. Taking his Educational Records Bureau exam in January, Karl spent much of the allotted time lecturing the test-givers on the architectural quirks of the Chrysler Building visible through the classroom window. (The urns jutting from the 29th floor, he is fond of pointing out, were modeled after the hood ornament on the 1929 Chrysler Plymouth.) Trying to summarize the erratic score that resulted, the E.R.B. made particular -- if rather stoic -- mention of Karl's "most noteworthy . . . fund of knowledge."

Of course, even without a standardized-test score, Karl's parents know he's a genius -- and they know that they should never, ever use that term.

3. Avoid calling your child a genius. "There are three reasons the label could only be unhelpful," says Dr. Jack Shonkoff, an expert on early childhood development. "One, it puts an enormous burden on the kid that he or she will have trouble living up to. Two, it's a setup for other people -- relatives, teachers -- to be disappointed in the kid's future performance. And three, it serves to set the child apart from other children. Extremely talented kids are pigeonholed enough as it is; the last thing they need is a label that ostracizes them further."

4. Don't expect your child to be popular. Combating social isolation may be the greatest challenge for those raising exceptionally intelligent kids. Karl has had a typically uphill battle finding a school -- let alone a circle of friends -- that can contain him. At 3 years old, he was asked to leave his preschool program at the local Y.M.C.A. when his obvious boredom rendered him, in his teacher's opinion, a bad influence on the other children. After a search, his parents discovered the East Manhattan School for Bright and Gifted Children, only to watch the independent school close its doors this winter. Karl has since transferred to a first-grade class at a public school in Brooklyn, where he was immediately promoted to its accelerated program. But his social life is lagging far behind.

It's no surprise. Highly gifted children tend to forge friendships the way adults do -- on the basis of shared interests and coincidental pursuits, rather than falling into packs according to grade. "These kids just aren't likely to be part of a huge gang in the lunchroom," Berger says. "The very best their parents can do is to try and help the child find one good friend."

5. Don't sacrifice educational advancement to give your child a "normal" upbringing. Holding children back from upper-level grades and early college not only won't help them socially, it will also frustrate them -- and their teachers. "These kids will exhaust the resources of any normal classroom," Berger says. "Six-, seven- and eight-year-olds who are interested in aerospace technology shouldn't be stuck in homeroom."

Karl's far-flung pursuits could exhaust just about anyone. Having dabbled at the piano since he was 3, he recently requested a violin, and his parents have managed to borrow one. The family's apartment is cluttered with Karl's drawings of the Titanic reimagined as a medieval galleon, with his floor sculpture of Moscow's St. Basil's Cathedral reconfigured as an ancient Irish church and with the whirling presence of Karl himself.

Spinning to present his well-illustrated, self-assigned report on the Statue of Liberty, he announces: "The architect was Frederic-Auguste Bartholdi; Auguste -- I mean -- did you hear that? A-goose. I said goose!" He bursts into giggles, and for the moment, at least, Karl Jr. is completely happy and 6 years old.

http://www.nytimes.com/2001/04/08/magazine/08GENIUS.html?pagewanted=print

9

WETWARE: THE BIOLOGICAL BASIS OF INTELLECTUAL GIFTEDNESS

Carolyn K

Why is "giftedness" such a puzzle for parents? Why is there so much confusion? The most common plea heard on TAGFAM is "my child is different; please help me understand why -- I think she's gifted."

The goal of this article is to introduce you to "wetware," the brain and its functions, and to help you understand, at the physical and biological level, the puzzle of the intellectually gifted child.

OK. Stay with me folks. In order to understand what comes later, we're going to have to wade through some tough territory for a few minutes.

If you're having trouble conceptualizing this stuff -- think in terms of what could happen if one of these areas of the brain was damaged or functioned suboptimally. Also, think in terms of how each of these areas contributes to the behaviors you see in your intellectually gifted child.

Is your child hypersensitive to smells? Tags in clothing? Does she have a terrific memory? How about physical coordination? Keep these "differences" in mind ... maybe you'll start to see the connection between brain structures and those little quirks of behavior that leave others wondering what planet this child is from.

Chemicals. When you think about it, intellectual giftedness is merely the fortunate happenstance of genetics as expressed in the chemical relationships in the brain. A nerve impulse here, a neurotransmitter there. Synapse, neuron, pathways. Memory, cognition, perception, instinct, emotion, creative thought -- these functions all start with chemical processes in the brain. These processes originate in the sequences of instructions encoded in your DNA. Intellectual giftedness begins with the creation of new life. Sperm meets egg. Bang! Life! All systems go! Another intellectually gifted human being is in the making.

Obviously, the functioning of the human brain is more than just a few chemical reactions. Development of the central nervous system begins as early as 16 days after conception and, by the sixth week, the neural tubes which later become the cerebral hemispheres are present in the

fetus. The cerebral cortex begins to develop by the 10th week. Thus, early in the pregnancy, chemical reactions and processes begin to define who and what we will be -- our genetic inheritance begins the process that gives rise to our intellectual abilities. For some, in utero exposure to toxins, stress, and other environmental factors will result in damage or other events which change, limit, or prevent the development of their full intellectual potential. Even before birth, the child's environment has a powerful influence upon the later expression of intellectual abilities.

Our understanding of the brain and how it functions has increased dramatically in the past two decades due to technological advances in diagnostic and imaging equipment. The development of Computer-Aided Tomography (CAT), Positron Emissions Tomography (PET), Magnetic Resonance Imaging (MRI) and other brain imaging techniques have made it possible for investigators to study the intact, whole, living human brain. Prior to the development of these techniques our understanding of the brain was limited and derived mainly from studies of individuals who had experienced loss or impairment of functionality due to disease, stroke, or physical injury. These types of studies have increased our knowledge of the anatomical structures of the brain (neuroanatomy) and the chemical processes by which it functions (neurochemistry).

Studies of stroke victims, in particular, allowed investigators to identify specific areas of the brain as being associated with certain behaviors or functions. More recent studies have shown that the brain is able to use cooperating groups of neurons in differing regions to accomplish a function or produce a behavior.

After the initial in utero growth of the human brain, there are normally growth spurts from ages 3 to 10 months, 2 to 4 years, 6 to 8 years, 10 to 12 years, and finally from 14 to 16 years of age. In addition to the physical growth process defined in the beginning by one's DNA, the brain undergoes physical changes related to exposure to environmental factors. The physical development of the brain benefits from some types of environmental factors, i.e. loving parents, good nutrition, interesting sensory stimuli and is harmed by others, i.e. exposure to lead or other toxic metals, child abuse, lack of physical contact with care givers . Both physical and social factors in the environment affect the brain's growth and development. Normal, healthy growth requires a supportive, loving, stimulating, and safe environment.

Next, we get into the really tough stuff. Stick with me, there are some treasures to be uncovered in what comes next!

Parts of The Brain and Related Systems

The central nervous system (CNS) is composed of the brain and the spinal cord. The peripheral nervous system sends sensory information to the CNS and sends motor commands from the CNS to the rest of the body. The autonomic nervous system sends nerve impulses to the body's internal organs. Sensory receptors in the peripheral organs (eyes, ears, skin, etc.) relay sensory information back to the CNS. The autonomic nervous system has other functions related to keeping the body's organs functioning in a balanced manner. [Aha! Maybe the "good" side of that annoying hypersensitivity is an increased ability to process sensory inputs.]

The overall structure of the brain is usually defined in terms of gray matter, the neuronal cell bodies, and white matter, primarily made up of myelinated neuronal axons. [You've been dying to know the difference, right?] The brain's "gray matter" makes up the cerebral cortex and the cerebellum (cerebellar cortex, and the subcortical cerebral and cerebellar nuclei). The cerebellum is involved in the control of muscles (motor movements) and posture adjustments. Because of its many connections to the cerebral cortex, it is possible that the cerebellum also plays a role in more complex brain functions (e.g. thinking).

The cerebral cortex is divided into four lobes: frontal, temporal, parietal, and occipital. Some neuroanatomists include the limbic system as a fifth lobe of the cerebral cortex. Within the cerebral cortex are regions which have been identified as the primary motor, primary sensory,

motor association and sensory association areas. These areas of the brain are responsible for the planning of motor activity, the interpretation of primary sensory inputs, and the organization of all the sensory and motor information that the brain receives from the nervous system.

The frontal cortex is the site of motor activation, intellect, conceptual planning, aspects of the personality, and aspects of language production.

Portions of the frontal cortex are involved in the movement of single muscles, the coordination of movement for groups of muscles, and the integration of primary sensory information. The temporal cortex is the seat the brain's memory, language, and emotion functions. The parietal cortex is the location of the association cortices for visual, tactile, and auditory input processing. The left parietal lobe is preferential in the processing of verbal information. The right parietal lobe is preferential in the processing of visual-spatial information. The occipital cortex is the primary sensory cortex for visual input.

The cerebral cortex is divided from front to back into left and right hemispheres. These hemispheres are connected by the corpus callosum and other small commissural tracts. In most humans, one of the two hemispheresis dominant and contains the area of the brain used to express language.

In 97% of the population, the left hemisphere is dominant; 99% of right

handed individuals and between 60% and 70% of left-handers are left-hemispheric dominant. Some individuals experience mixed dominance for handedness and others experience mixed dominance for language. There are tests which involve sensory inputs, either hearing or vision, that can be used to determine which hemisphere is dominant. Persons who have a dominant left hemisphere have a right ear advantage (hear better).

For vision the right visual field has an advantage for verbal inputs and the left visual field has an advantage for spatial input when the left hemisphere is dominant. For right hemisphere dominance the advantages are reversed, right for left, e.g. left ear, right eye for spatial, and left eye for verbal.

Studies of individuals who have experienced brain damage have led to the development of several theories about hemispheric function. A good book to read on this topic is "Left-Brain/Right-Brain." The left hemisphere is thought to be the seat of rational thought, analytic thinking, sequencing, abstracting, and logistical abilities. The right hemisphere is thought to be the seat of perceptual, visual-spatial, artistic, musical, and synthetic activity. The right hemisphere is also thought to be involved in both the perception and expression of affect (emotion) and the perception of social cues in the environment. More recent studies have shown that while these generalizations hold in most cases, there is increasing evidence of exceptions. [In other words, the information about left and right hemisphericity is probably true but don't bet the farm on it.]

The major function of the limbic system is memory. Earlier suppositions held that the limbic system was the primary seat of one's emotions.

Two components of the limbic system, the hippocampus and the amygdalia, play critical roles in learning and memory. The amygdalia is also thought to play a role in the integration of memories and facial recognition and social behavior. Two types of memory have been postulated by researches: working memory (short-term) and consolidated memory (long-term). Short term memory is thought to involve neurochemical changes at specific synapses. Long term memory is thought to arise from the synthesis of new protein molecules which create permanent changes in the brain's synaptic architecture. [Oh! So that's why the two are different ...]

Defining Intellectual Giftedness

Intellectual giftedness is "mental quickness and mental flexibility."

Developmental delays or developmental precociousness affect the expression of one's intellectual abilities. Environmental influences can enhance or retard maturation. Physical development of the brain and development of brain functions can be significantly and irreversibly affected by physical trauma or environmental factors. Some children are more intellectually capable than their age-mates due to a combination of factors, both physical and environmental. Environment can't give the child more than he started with physically; it can, however, adversely affect the development of the brain. Differences in intellectual capacity or expressions of behaviors seem to arise from the complex interplay between what you start with, the environment influences the child experiences, and the child's individual developmental patterns.

Hopefully, the above explanations have the set the stage for the assertion that there is only one type of giftedness -- intellectual giftedness.

There is a clearly defined biological basis for the development of "superior" intellectual abilities. The label "superior," however, is a value judgement placed upon the expression of those abilities as specific behaviors. There are other more popular definitions of giftedness in use but these appear to appear to be more a description of certain behaviors which are held in high esteem in our culture. Definition by description is, perhaps, a valid way of looking at the issue of giftedness.

But, does a definition based upon shifting cultural norms help us to understand the needs and abilities of intellectually gifted children?

I think not.

http://www.hoagiesgifted.org/montage/v1n4p3.html

10

A PSYCHOLOGICAL AUTOPSY OF BOBBY FISCHER

Joseph G. Ponterotto

Chess player Bobby Fischer's tortured life illustrates why promising young talents deserve better support programs.

At a 1958 tournament in Yugoslavia, Mikhail Tal, a legendary attacking grandmaster and one-time world champion, mocked chess prodigy Bobby Fischer for being "cuckoo." Tal's taunting may have been a deliberate attempt to rattle Fischer, then just 15 but already a major force in the highly competitive world of high-level chess.

But others from that world — including a number of grandmasters who'd spent time with him — thought Fischer not just eccentric, but deeply troubled. At a tournament in Bulgaria four years later, U.S. grandmaster Robert Byrne suggested that Fischer see a psychiatrist, to which Fischer replied that "a psychiatrist ought to pay [me] for the privilege of working on [my] brain." According to journalist Dylan Loeb McClain, Hungarian-born grandmaster Pal Benko commented, "I am not a psychiatrist, but it was obvious he was not normal. ... I told him, 'You are paranoid,' and he said that 'paranoids can be right.'"

Robert James Fischer passed away of kidney failure at the age of 64 in January 2008 in his adopted home of Reykjavik, Iceland, where, 36 years earlier, he had captivated the world with his stunning defeat of Boris Spassky, the reigning world chess champion from Russia. As the first North American to win the world title after a half-century of Russian domination, Fischer gained enduring worldwide fame.

By almost all accounts a brilliant mind, Fischer was perhaps the most visionary chess player since José Raul Capablanca, a Cuban who held the world title for six years in the 1920s. Fischer's innovative, daring play — at age 13, he defeated senior master (and former U.S. Open champion) Donald Byrne in what is sometimes called "The Game of the Century" — made him a hero figure to millions in the United States and throughout the world. In 1957, Fischer became the youngest winner of the U.S. chess championship — he was just 14 — before going on to beat Spassky for the world title in 1972.

But Fischer forfeited that title just three years later, refusing to defend his crown under rules proposed by the World Chess Federation, and he played virtually no competitive chess in ensuing decades, retreating, instead, into isolation and seeming paranoia. Because of a series of rankly anti-Semitic public utterances and his praise, on radio, for the Sept. 11, 2001 attack on the World Trade Center, at his death, Fischer was seen by much of the world as spoiled, arrogant and mean-spirited.

In recent years, however, researchers have come to understand that Bobby Fischer was psychologically troubled from early childhood. Careful examination of his life and family shows that he likely suffered with mental illness that may never have been properly diagnosed or treated.

Any psychological evaluation of a person who is not alive must, of course, include a great deal of qualification. But the psychological history of America's greatest chess champion clearly raises two profound questions, one specific to Fischer and chess and the other more general: What would Bobby Fischer's life and career have looked like had he received appropriate mental health services throughout his life? And is there a way for society to help troubled, often defiant prodigies become less troubled, without diminishing their genius and eventual contribution to society?

To understand Bobby Fischer's psychological makeup, it is important to understand his personal history, which began on March 9, 1943, when he was born in Chicago to Regina Wender, a Swiss native of Polish-Jewish heritage, and, most likely, Paul Felix Nemenyi, a Hungarian-born and -trained mechanical engineer who met Regina in 1942. He was also Jewish. (Hans Gerhardt Fischer, a German-born biophysicist whom Regina married in Moscow in 1933, is listed as Fischer's father on his birth certificate, but FBI records released after Regina's death and other documentation make it all but certain that Nemenyi was the biological father.)

Bobby had an older sister, Joan, born to Regina and Hans Gerhardt Fischer in 1937 in Moscow, where the couple was living at the time. Soon after Joan's birth, the marriage between Hans Gerhardt and Regina began to fail, and in 1939, Regina and Joan came to the United States without him. He never entered the U.S. and by all accounts was totally absent in the lives of the Fischer children. In 1945, Regina legally divorced him.

Soon after Bobby's birth, Regina Fischer moved the family from Chicago to Pullman, Wash., where Paul Nemenyi was then living, then to Moscow, Idaho, on to Portland, Ore., then south to Los Angeles, and on to the tiny town of Mobile, in the Arizona desert about 35 miles southwest of Phoenix. According to Frank Brady's classic biography of Fischer, Profile of a Prodigy, Regina took odd jobs to support her family until eventually gaining employment as a teacher in Los Angeles and Mobile.

From Arizona, the Fischer family moved to Brooklyn, N.Y., in 1949, where Regina, already a registered nurse, pursued a master's degree in nursing education at New York University. When Bobby was 6, his sister bought him an inexpensive chess set from a candy store, and together they learned the moves. Bobby had always liked games and puzzles, and initially his interest in chess was unremarkable, as he reflected years later to Brady: "At first it was just a game like any other, only a little more complicated."

It appears Fischer never adjusted well to the New York City school system. He was expelled from a public school in Manhattan when he kicked the principal, and he dropped out of high school. In contrast to this disinterest in school, Bobby developed an intense focus on chess. In fact, to say Bobby became obsessed with chess would be a wild understatement.

During Bobby's childhood and early adolescence, Regina consulted with, or had Bobby meet directly, three different mental health professionals. According to Brady, Regina spoke with Ariel Mengarini, a New York City psychiatrist and chess master, about curbing her son's "chess obsession," and Mengarini responded: "I could think of a lot worse things than chess that a person could devote himself to and ... you should let him find his own way." Regina received a similar response from Harold Kline, who saw her son at the Children's Psychiatric Division of the Brooklyn Jewish Hospital.

World-renowned chess grandmaster and psychoanalyst Dr. Reuben Fine noted in his book, Bobby Fischer's Conquest of the World's Chess Championship, that Regina consulted with him soon after her son won the 1956 U.S junior championship at the age of 13. "He came to see me about half a dozen times," Fine wrote. "Each time we played chess for an hour or two. In order to maintain a relationship with him, I had to win, which I did. ... My family remembers how furious he was after each encounter, muttering that I was 'lucky.' Hopeful that I might help him to develop in other directions, I started a conversation at one point about what he was doing in school. As soon as school was mentioned, he became furious, screamed, 'You have tricked me,' and promptly walked out. For years afterward, whenever I met him in clubs or tournaments he gave me angry looks, as though I had done him some immeasurable harm by trying to get a little closer to him."

This exaggerated, perhaps paranoid reaction to Fine's overture reflects a pattern in Bobby Fischer's interpersonal style that would be a hallmark of both his adolescent and adult behavior.

But according to the recollections of both Brady and Fischer's brother-in-law, Russell Targ, Bobby never engaged in long-term psychotherapy with any mental health professional.

As Bobby grew into adolescence, he clashed with his mother frequently and directly. According to BBC journalists David Edmonds and John Eidinow, who wrote a book about Fischer, eventually Bobby and Regina could no longer live together, and in the fall of 1960, when Bobby was 17, she moved out of their Brooklyn apartment to live with a female friend in the Bronx. In an interview with journalist Ralph Ginzburg in August 1961, Bobby discussed the circumstances of his break from his mother.

Fischer: "After that [becoming an international grandmaster in 1958], I quit school."

Ginzburg: "How did your mother feel about that?"

Fischer: "She and I just don't see eye to eye together. She's a square. She keeps telling me that I'm too interested in chess, that I should get friends outside of chess, you can't make a living from chess, that I should finish high school and all that nonsense. She keeps in my hair, and I don't like people in my hair, you know, so I had to get rid of her."

This "break" was, in fact, anything but permanent or complete; Fischer and his mother would have an on-and-off relationship throughout his life. (Interestingly, as Bobby lay critically ill in a Reykjavik hospital, he was thinking of his mother, his brother-in-law wrote in his 2008 autobiography, Do You See What I See?)

According to Brady, the Fischer biographer, his mother was a concerned and devoted parent but could be domineering. It was clear she was highly talented, well educated and multilingual; in fact, after her children were on their own, Regina returned to Germany to finish medical school, earning both a medical degree and an eventual doctorate in hematology.

But raising Joan and Bobby as a single immigrant parent in the 1940s and 1950s was challenging, and Regina was constantly short of money. "Regina was financially desperate, so much so that, through a Jewish charity, she attempted to place her daughter, Joan, with another family," Edmonds and Eidinow wrote. But this arrangement fell through, the foster mother asking Regina to take Joan back. Interestingly, the foster mother became suspicious of Regina, having seen chemical formulas on documents that she had left among her daughter's belongings, and reported her to the FBI, which in 1942 began surveillance that would last three decades.

It is not surprising that the FBI would investigate the foster mother's report about the chemical formulas. It was early in the Cold War, and Bobby's mother and presumed father at the time, Hans Gerhardt Fischer, had lived in Russia for an extended period of time; both had high-level scientific training. The resulting FBI reports on Regina Fischer and the two men in her life, Hans Gerhardt Fischer and Paul Felix Nemenyi, reveal no espionage. But they do shed light on the unusual psychology and behavior of the mother of America's greatest chess prodigy.

According to various entries in the FBI reports, eventually made public by journalists and biographers, Regina was bright and articulate but difficult to deal with. Soon after Bobby's birth, Regina received a mandated mental health evaluation after being arrested for disturbing the peace in an incident that occurred when Regina and baby Bobby lived at a Chicago charity for indigent single mothers , the Hackett Memorial Home. After Joan's foster arrangement fell through, Regina tried to sneak her into the facility, even though she'd been told there was no room for another child.

In its evaluation, the Chicago-based Municipal Psychiatric Institute diagnosed Regina as a "stilted (paranoid) personality, querulent [sic] but not psychotic." The FBI apparently also thought her troubled. According to FBI reports, the bureau, at one point, felt it had exhausted the usefulness of clandestine surveillance of Regina, noting, "It appears the only logical investigation remaining would be an interview of the subject, but due to her mental instability, this line of action is not recommended."

Regina Fischer had ambivalent feelings toward her son's chess career. Early on, she encouraged Bobby to broaden his interest and friendship base beyond chess. As Bobby's genius for chess became more apparent, however, Regina did all she could to support his passion. She was often involved in protests and demonstrations relating to Bobby's chess career and U.S. chess in general. In 1960, for example, she picketed the White House because the State Department refused the national chess team's request to play in the 1960 Chess Olympiad in East Germany. Interestingly, the person now alive who knew Regina and Bobby best, her son-in-law Russell Targ, remarked to me that "Bobby would never have become world champion without Regina."

Regina Fischer died of cancer in 1997 at the age of 84 in Palo Alto, Calif. Bobby's older sister Joan died of a cerebral hemorrhage a year later. These two losses, coming so close in time, would have a significant impact on Bobby's developing psychological state.

With Regina's death, her 750-page FBI file became publicly available. The first to read it were former Philadelphia Inquirer reporters Peter Nicholas and Clea Benson, and their investigative research is groundbreaking. A critical finding gleaned from the FBI report concerns the identity of Bobby's biological father. Though we cannot be 100 percent certain without genetic testing, there is a plethora of convincing documentary evidence — from the FBI file and from elsewhere — that Paul Felix Nemenyi, rather than Hans Gerhardt Fischer, was Bobby's biological father. At what point Bobby came to know the truth about his father is unclear. Suffice it to say, whether or when Bobby learned of his biological father's identity would also have implications for his sense of identity and psychological development.

From early childhood, Bobby Fischer was fiercely independent, eccentric and lacking in conventional social skills. Contemporaries often felt his conduct went beyond mere eccentricity. In his book on Fischer, psychoanalyst Reuben Fine reflected that for many years "chess players approached me with the request to try to help Bobby out of his personal problems. In spite of his genius, he was socially awkward, provocative, argumentative and unhappy."

Bobby's inner turmoil and frustration would at times erupt into violence. Mike Franett, writing for BobbyFischer.net in 2000, interviewed former Fischer friend and chess master Ron Gross, who described a car trip in 1957 when Bobby, sitting in the back seat, seriously bit fellow chess player Gil Ramirez on the arm. Gross reported that the bite marks were visible years after the incident. Later in his life , Bobby would also act out violently when, according to journalist Ivan Solotaroff, he assaulted a former Worldwide Church of God member who he felt had betrayed his trust.

Journalists Nicholas and Benson describe a meeting at the Marshall Chess Club in New York City in the late 1950s during which Bobby's emotional stability was discussed by the club's board of governors. "[N]o one doubted the teenager's talent. But his prickly behavior was alienating some of the wealthy sponsors whose support he would need to rise to the top," Nicholas and Benson wrote. "'Some of what he did was so outrageous it was decided maybe he had emotional problems,' says [Allen] Kaufman, [a chess master and Fischer friend] who attended the meeting. What to do? Board members talked about finding a psychiatrist. They considered Reuben Fine, himself one of the giants of the game. Then someone raised a question: What if therapy worked? What if treatment sapped Fischer's drive to win , depriving the United States of its first homegrown world champ? Meeting adjourned. No one, Kaufman recalls, wanted to tamper with that finely tuned brain."

Grandmasters Robert Byrne and Pal Benko told Bobby directly that he should consider seeing a psychiatrist. Their comments are supported by observations of odd behavior made throughout Bobby's life . In his New York Times obituary of Fischer, Bruce Weber noted that the chess champion made "outlandish demands on tournament directors — for special lighting, special seating, special conditions to ensure quiet. He complained that opponents were trying to poison his food, that his hotel rooms were bugged, that Russians were colluding at tournaments and prearranging draws. He began to fear flying because he thought the Russians might hide booby traps on the plane."

For his book, Searching for Bobby Fischer, which was made into a motion picture, Fred Waitzkin interviewed Gross, who shared the following memories of a fishing trip to Ensenada, Mexico: "He looked terrible … clothes all baggy, wearing old beat-up shoes. … Then I noticed that he was favoring his mouth, and he told me that he'd had some work done on his teeth; he'd had a dentist take all the fillings out of his mouth. … I said 'Bobby, that's going to ruin your teeth. Did you have him put plastic in the holes?' And he said, 'I didn't have anything put in. I don't want anything artificial in my head.' He'd read about a guy wounded in World War II who had a metal plate in his head that was always picking up vibrations, maybe even radio transmissions. He said the same thing could happen from metal in your teeth."

After winning the world chess championship in 1972, Bobby lapsed into a period of isolation and growing paranoia, manifested primarily in virulent and vitriolic anti-Semitism and anti-Americanism. These rants could be heard on radio broadcasts Bobby made in the Philippines and Hungary. Of course, Bobby's mother and his probable father, Nemenyi, were Jewish. Edmonds and Eidinow, the BBC journalists, wondered whether some of the roots in Bobby's hatred of Jews stemmed from rejection of his mother. In his 2003 mini-biography of Bobby, former 15-year world chess champion Garry Kasparov suggested Bobby's anti-Semitism might be related to his conflicts with Jewish-American grandmaster Samuel Reshevsky, as well as his dislike of other Jews involved in the chess community, including wealthy sponsors and journalists. Kasparov adds another interesting observation: "I think Fischer's anti-Semitism mania, which increased with the years, was largely associated with the domination of 'Soviet-Jewish' players. It seemed to him that they were all united against him with the aim of preventing him from becoming world champion. I remember Reshevsky telling me how, during the Interzonal tournament on Palma de Mallorca, with burning eyes Fischer informed him that he was reading a 'very interesting book.' 'What is it?' Sammy asked innocently. 'Mein Kampf!' Bobby replied."

Regardless of the origins of Bobby's unspeakable anti-Semitism, his anti-Jewish rantings, in time, alienated the majority of former allies, friends and supporters. That's to say nothing of his comments following the terror attacks of Sept. 11, 2001, made via a radio station in the Philippines. According to a 2002 Rene Chun article in The Atlantic Monthly, Fischer announced, "This is all wonderful news. I applaud the act. The U.S. and Israel have been slaughtering the Palestinians, just slaughtering them for years. Robbing them and slaughtering them. Nobody gave a shit. Now it's coming back to the U.S. Fuck the U.S. I want to see the U.S. wiped out."

The goal of a psychological autopsy is to assess the feelings, thoughts, behaviors and relationships of an individual who is dead. Such an evaluation is usually conducted without the benefit of direct observation, but often with more access to historical records and archives than would be available in a standard psychological assessment.

Check out the move-by-move re-enactment of "The Game of the Century" — Donald Byrne vs. Bobby Fischer, 1956

Bobby Fischer was not a patient of mine, and I have not had access to any mental health records on him or his mother, save for those uncovered by journalists who obtained FBI files under the Freedom of Information Act. It is inappropriate of me to proffer a formal psychological diagnosis of Fischer, and in writing this assessment, I am guided by the ethical code of the American Psychological Association, which says that practitioners in my position should "document the efforts they made and the result of those efforts, clarify the probable impact of their limited information on the reliability and validity of their opinions, and appropriately limit the nature and extent of their conclusions or recommendations."

With those qualifications and limits well in mind, I have come to believe Bobby had a genetic vulnerability to develop a mental illness, and that this predisposition — in concert with early life trauma and the burden of relentless media pressure — eventually led to serious mental health problems. My mental-illness hypotheses should be considered speculative and in need of independent scrutiny from other mental health professionals, who, in time, will have access to expanded archival documentation on the life of Fischer and his family.

Still, enough is known about Bobby Fischer's life and family history — including the mental health history of his relatives — for me to reach some general conclusions.

Bobby's likely biological father, Paul Nemenyi, was highly intelligent, an established mechanical engineer and technical author who, at one point, collaborated with Albert Einstein's son, Hans Albert Einstein, on hydrology theory. But after emigrating from Hungary to the U.S. in 1939, Nemenyi had trouble adjusting, and at least a couple of his colleagues thought quite negatively of his character.

Nicholas and Benson uncovered documents in which Nemenyi was described as "an unstable and undesirable person" by a committee member of the Emergency Committee in Aid of Displaced Foreign Scholars and as "a misfit" by fellow Hungarian immigrant Theodore von Karman, a respected aeronautical scientist. Nicholas and Benson wrote that Nemenyi's colleagues told them that he always walked around with soap in his pockets, frequently washed his hands and was very careful not to touch door handles. He also had an aversion to wool and would go to work in the winter with his pajamas sticking out from underneath his clothes because, he said, he was layering to keep warm.

According to the FBI files, staffers at Jewish Family Services in Los Angeles, with whom Nemenyi was sharing his concerns about the mental health of Regina and Bobby in 1947, reported that the "agency did not completely trust Nemenyi, as they considered him somewhat of a 'paranoid type.'" The information on Nemenyi is limited, and the assertions in documents uncovered by Nicholas and Benson do not constitute definitive evidence of mental disorder.

The available anecdotal psychiatric evidence on Regina Fischer is more detailed. As I noted earlier, Regina's FBI file documented a diagnosis of "stilted (paranoid) personality, querulent [sic] but not psychotic." This diagnosis reflected the parlance of the mid-1940s and would be considered outdated today. Using the terminology of the current revision of the Diagnostic and Statistical Manual of Mental Disorders, Regina Fischer exhibited traits consistent with paranoid personality disorder, a non-psychotic mental illness. (Keep in mind, however, that Regina had good reason to be suspicious; she was, in fact, kept under surveillance by the FBI for roughly three decades. And, according to Regina's son-in-law, Russell Targ, the ongoing FBI surveillance hindered her ability to find steady employment.)

Assuming Nemenyi to be Fischer's biological father, the chess champion had two half-siblings: a sister, Joan, born to Regina Fischer and Hans Gerhardt Fischer, and a brother, Peter, who was born to Bobby's likely biological father, Nemenyi, and his wife. Like his father Paul, Peter was a gifted intellectual; he earned his doctorate in mathematics from Princeton and authored a respected book on statistics. According to Nicholas and Benson, however, Peter's "end was unhappy. Sick with prostate cancer, he killed himself [in 2002]. He had been living alone in a Durham, N.C., apartment crammed with statistics papers. Friends say they often spotted him pushing a collection of shopping baskets around town, wearing oven mitts for gloves." Again, there is not enough evidence to be confident of Peter Nemenyi's mental state throughout his life, but in his final years it was certainly problematic.

I have found no information suggesting that Joan, Bobby's half-sister, suffered from any mental disorder. In fact, it is clear that Joan was a reliable and consistent source of support for her brother, and it appears Bobby was as close to his big sister as he could be, given his interpersonal difficulties, general mistrust of others and paranoid tendencies.

It is my clinical intuition that Joan's death, coming only a year after their mother's passing, was a devastating loss to Bobby. His own grief process was further complicated: He could attend neither his mother's nor his sister's funeral for a very realistic fear that he would be arrested on arrival in the U.S. because of his violation of U.S. sanctions against Yugoslavia when he played his rematch against Spassky there in 1992.

A variety of authors have speculated about Bobby Fischer's mental state. For example, Valery Krylov, a specialist in the "psycho-physiological rehabilitation of sportsmen," who is cited in Garry Kasparov's mini-biography of Fischer, believed Bobby suffered from schizophrenia. Krylov had worked with former world chess champion Anatoly Karpovf or two decades and arrived at his diagnostic conclusion based on an examination of correspondence to and from Fischer, and published articles related to Fischer. A more recent and popular diagnosis surfacing in the literature suggests that Bobby suffered from Asperger's Disorder.

In attempting to enhance the reliability and validity of a psychological assessment, clinicians form "differential diagnoses" that help to screen in and screen out potential "best bets" through a systematic, decision-tree process. In hypothesizing about Bobby's mental status, a differential diagnosis could include the Asperger's Disorder and schizophrenia (paranoid type) just mentioned, as well as paranoid personality disorder and delusional disorder.

Providing a detailed differential diagnosis of Bobby Fischer would require a much longer treatment of the topic than is possible here. I do provide such an expanded consideration in a book-length project in progress. For present purposes, suffice it to say that I believe Bobby did not meet all the necessary criteria to reach diagnoses of schizophrenia or Asperger's Disorder. The evidence is stronger for paranoid personality disorder, which the Diagnostic and Statistical Manual of Mental Disorders (DSM) says "may be first apparent in childhood and adolescence with solitariness, poor peer relationships, social anxiety, underachievement in school, hypersensitivity, peculiar thoughts and language, and idiosyncratic fantasies. These children may appear to be 'odd' or 'eccentric' and attract teasing."

In addition to paranoid behavior, in adulthood, Fischer clearly manifested the kind of non-bizzare delusions characteristic of the persecutory type of delusional disorder, which the DSM describes this way: "[T]he central theme of the delusion involves the person's belief that he or she is being conspired against, cheated, spied on, followed, poisoned or drugged, maliciously maligned, harassed, or obstructed in the pursuit of long-term goals. Small slights may be exaggerated and become the focus of a delusional system. The focus of the delusion is often on some injustice that must be remedied by legal action ('querulous paranoia'), and the affected person may engage in repeated attempts to obtain satisfaction by appeal to the courts and other government agencies. Individuals with persecutory delusions are often resentful and angry and may resort to violence against those they believe are hurting them."

This DSM language appears to describe Bobby's later life with a high degree of accuracy. Bobby did experience delusions that the Jews were out to destroy him, he was often involved in filing lawsuits (none of which he won), and he did turn violent on at least three occasions.

So my hypothesis about the course of Bobby Fischer's mental illness can be summarized in this way: Bobby's family history — particularly his mother's possible mental illness — modestly predisposed him to paranoid personality disorder. Bobby had no father figure and perhaps did not even know who his real father was until later in life; he was raised by a single mother experiencing financial hardships and daily stress from FBI surveillance. These circumstances added to Bobby's level of psychosocial stress and increased his vulnerability to mental illness. The stress and vulnerability were further magnified by his celebrity status and the unremitting media pressure that accompanied it.

As Bobby moved out of regular tournament play in the 1970s, he isolated himself, and his paranoia intensified. In some ways, the structure, demands and focus of chess tournaments may have confined or contained his paranoid thoughts and behaviors. In

1973, in what now seems almost a prophetic statement, Reuben Fine wrote, "Chess seems to have been the best therapy in the world for him."

The psychosocial stressors on Bobby intensified in the 1980s and 1990s. He was named in an arrest warrant the State Department issued in connection with his Yugoslavia "rematch" with Spassky; he suffered the untimely loss of his mother and sister; he was arrested in Japan in 2004 in connection with the 1992 warrant; and he struggled for years to find a safe haven from U.S. arrest, finding one only in 2005, when he was granted full Icelandic citizenship. These varied and intense psychosocial stressors contributed to the presence of non-bizzare, persecutory delusions that were superimposed on a pre-existing paranoid personality disorder.

Over the half century since Regina Fischer first brought her son to the Children's Psychiatric Division of Brooklyn Jewish Hospital, the fields of psychology and psychiatry have advanced considerably. If Bobby Fischer had been born in this decade, he and his family would, at least in theory, have access to a variety of psychological assessments and interventions.

First, the daily stress Regina Fischer suffered as a subject of FBI surveillance could have been reduced with appropriate treatment. She might have received supportive and cognitive-behavioral counseling to help her develop coping strategies for dealing with that stress, and she might also have gained access to legal or financial support from civil liberties groups. Given Bobby's temperament, Regina could have benefited from parent training and support programs. Bobby's sister Joan might have benefited from personal counseling, given the burdens of her responsibility for troubled relatives. And clearly, family counseling — something far more likely to occur today than in the 1940s, particularly with working-class families — could have helped the Fischers as a group.

If the hypothesis posited in this article is correct — that Bobby suffered from a genetically predisposed paranoid personality disorder — he could today receive treatment that includes the long-term individual psychotherapy often required to make progress with patients exhibiting paranoid symptoms. Generally speaking, such patients are difficult to treat, given their mistrust of the therapist and therapy process.

With regard to schooling, a 21st-century Bobby Fischer would likely receive special support services, including individual and group counseling, which he probably did not receive at Public School 3, from which he was expelled, or at Brooklyn's Erasmus Hall High School, from which he voluntarily dropped out at age 16. Too little is known about Bobby's day-to-day behavior and affective state in elementary or high school to confidently recommend a particular medication regimen. But depending on the presence and intensity of coexisting symptoms — anxiety, depression and attention deficits in some subject areas — Bobby might well be prescribed a psychotropic medication.

And even though Bobby had an ambivalent relationship with his mother, he certainly could have used intensive grief and support counseling in 1997 and 1998, when his mother and sister passed away. Regina and Joan were Bobby's lifelong advocates, and despite his struggles and challenges, he felt emotionally close to them.

Would Bobby Fischer have become a world chess champion if he had been involved in long-term individual psychotherapy, family therapy and special support services and, possibly, been prescribed a psychotropic medication? This question I cannot answer.

Perhaps psychological intervention and the structure it provides would have stabilized Bobby's life and chess career. Psychological treatment could have equipped him with stress- and media-management coping skills; it could have provided techniques to bring his cognitive distortions and anti-Semitism under more control; it could have given him insight into his family history; and it could have supported him in developing and maintaining friendships and romantic partners.

If this cadre of interventions were successful, even in part, Bobby Fischer might very well have been world chess champion for a decade, rather than just three years, and a much happier person throughout his life .

But there is also the possibility that psychological intervention might have distracted Bobby from his chess focus and sapped the drive — the almost superhuman focus — that is a hallmark of genius. And this possibility is at the center of the larger question that Bobby Fischer's troubled life raises: What can be done to help our most brilliant and talented citizens get the mental health treatment they need and deserve while ensuring that genius is not suppressed in the process?

Unfortunately, Bobby Fischer's dramatic rise to world pre-eminence and equally dramatic descent into isolation and mental instability is a life path not unique to him or to chess. To be sure, Paul Morphy, the New Orleans chess prodigy who played a century earlier than Bobby, also lapsed into a state of delusion, in his case centered on belief that he was being persecuted by his brother-in-law, the executor of his father's estate. But outside the field of chess, one can find countless examples of prodigies who succumbed to stress and intense career expectations. The musical genius of Michael Jackson, the acting and singing gift of Judy Garland, and the poetry and prose brilliance of Sylvia Plath represent but a few examples of promising talent undermined by mental health problems insufficiently dealt with, or left untended altogether.

Part of the psychological challenge for American "genius," in particular, lies in this country's cultural value system. It's a system that places high emphasis on individualism and individual accomplishment, rather than group effort. The chess, math or piano prodigy senses early on the extreme pride that family members, coaches and teachers have in his or her "unique" ability. At the same time, the prodigy also may learn that he or she will be excused for untoward behavior because adults are reluctant to take any action that might slow or derail the development of a "star." But that prospective star will likely also understand, very early on, the downside of life as a prodigy: Acclaim and special privileges continue only as long as genius shines.

Given stable childhoods and average genetic predispositions for dealing with stress, many prodigies manage such pressures well and become successful in their fields while achieving at least a semblance of life balance. Some prodigies, however — including Bobby Fischer, who had an unstable early family life, the pressure of early fame and, perhaps, a genetic tendency toward psychological difficulties — are not equipped to navigate life's challenges without counseling intervention.

I won't try here to describe all the programs and interventions that might foster psychological health in young people with special talents. Instead, I offer a brief outline of two primary areas in which early intervention could create better chances for our gifted and talented to achieve balanced lives.

Compared to young people who are identified, early on, as being at risk for learning disabilities or emotional-behavioral problems — to give just two of many possible challenges — children who have special intellectual or artistic talents are often assumed to be OK, psychologically, so long as their general academic performance is satisfactory. Because of their gifts, they are often left to their own devices and given few or no special support services.

Because the pressures on the exceedingly gifted are obvious and too often debilitating or deadly, I suggest that schools take formal steps to identify talented students early on and then to provide them with support systems that promote their special talent while, simultaneously, helping them connect with other spheres of academic and social life. Such support services could include individual counseling, parent training, and support and group counseling with other gifted students.

I also favor the creation of mentoring — or "big brother" and "big sister" — programs for extremely gifted children. At an awards show last fall, young musical sensation Justin Bieber thanked an older friend — Usher, who'd also been a musical phenomenon at an early age — for acting as his mentor on professional, personal and life-balance issues. Such one-on-one mentoring can be very beneficial to young talents as they learn to navigate the challenges a life of high expectations and achievement poses, and I see no reason schools can't be more active in encouraging such pairings. There is already a wide literature on programs for gifted and talented youth and adolescents, and this is a critical area for continued research. But in some cases, at least, it may well take a genius to help a genius in the making.

http://www.psmag.com/culture/a-psychological-autopsy-of-bobby-fischer-25959/

11

16 OF THE SMARTEST CHILDREN IN HISTORY

Vivian Giang

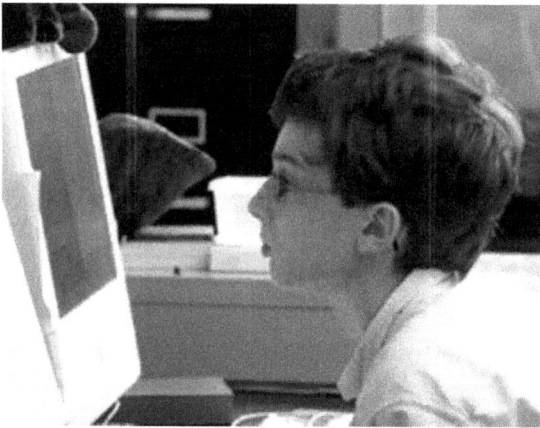

At the age most of us were playing with food and discovering our toes, child prodigies around the globe are learning complex languages and studying fields we've never heard of.

Many of these children went on to do great things. Others were crippled by emotional instability. Some have great potential and are just getting started.

Wolfgang Amadeus Mozart—The six-year-old composer

Wikimedia Commons

At the age of three, Wolfgang Mozart played the harpsichord and by six, he had written his first musical composition. This was followed by the first symphony at the age of eight and opera at 12.

The legendary composer's musical talents were quickly discovered shortly after his birth in Salzburg, Austria in 1756.

As a five-year-old, Mozart performed at the University of Salzburg with the piano and at the imperial court in Vienna the next year. At the age of 14, he set out to Italy to become an opera composer.

He died at the age of 35 and left behind more than 600 composed pieces.

William Rowan Hamilton—Multilingual by the age of five

Wikimedia Commons

Born in Dublin, Ireland in 1805, William Rowan Hamilton showed his intellectual abilities at an early age, mastering Latin, Greek and Hebrew by the age of five.

By the time he was 13, the future mathematician knew 13 different languages, including Sanscrit, Persian, Italian, Arabic, Syriac and Indian dialects.

At the age of 15, Hamilton found errors while studying the works of French mathematician Pierre-Simon, marquis de Laplace.

He was appointed Professor of Astronomy, Director of the Dunsink Observatory and the Royal Astronomer of Ireland while he was still studying as a university student.

His greatest contributions includes a theory of dynamics and quaternions, a method used for three-dimensional space in mathematics.

Ireland's greatest mathematician was knighted in 1835 and died in 1865.

Pablo Picasso—The greatest artist of the 20th century

Sim_ via flickr

Born in Spain in 1881, Pablo Picasso developed his skills early, producing complex pieces with the support of his artist father and by the age of 15, his first large oil painting The First Communion was displayed in Barcelona.

The following year, his painting Science and Charity won a gold medal in Malaga and received honorable mention at a national exhibit for the fine arts in Madrid.

His interest in modern art eventually caused a rift between him and his parents.

In the early 20th century, Picasso co-founded the Cubist movement. His technique and style would change often throughout his life.

The artist died in France in 1973.

William James Sidis—The smartest man who ever lived

Wikimedia Commons

At eight years old, William James Sidis proved his mathematics giftedness by developing a new logarithm table based on the number 12 and gave a lecture at Harvard University a year later. The child genius set the world record as the youngest person to enroll at the prestigious university at the age of 11 and graduated cum laude five years later.

Sidis is considered to be the smartest man who ever lived, by some, with an estimated IQ of 250-300.

Before his own experience with the terrible twos, Sidis had taught himself to read and shortly thereafter, became fluent in eight languages and wrote four original works of his own by the age of seven.

After an incredible childhood – or lack of it – adulthood was a struggle for Sidis and newspapers at the time reported that his "genius had burned out" due to the numerous obscure blue collared jobs he obtained throughout his life.

Shakuntala Devi—The "Hindu Mathematical Wizardess"

RussiaToday via YouTube

Born in 1939 in Bangalore, India to a lion tamer father, Shakuntala Devi started her relationship with numbers through card tricks she played with her father at the age of three.

Nicknamed the "Human Computer," and "Hindu Mathematical Wizardess" Devi demonstrated her mathematics abilities at the University of Mysore and Annamalai University as a child.

Her talent has been mentioned in the Guinness Book of World Records several times, such as when she extracted the 23rd root of a 201-digit number mentally and when she found the cube root of 332,812,557 in seconds.

In 2006, she published "In the Wonderland of Numbers," a story about a girl fascinated with digits.

Robert James Fischer—The greatest chess player

Da Nes via flickr

At 14-years-old, Robert "Bobby" Fischer won the World Chess Championship becoming the youngest winner of the title. In that year, he captured the attention of the chess world with what has since been dubbed as "The Game of the Century."

He broke another record the following year when he became the youngest international grandmaster of all times at the age of 15.

In 1972, he became the highest rated player in history with an FIDE rating of 2785.

In 1992, he played a match against an old rival in Yugoslavia and violated a United Nations sanction. Fischer dodged authorities for the next 12 years until his capture in Japan in 2004. He was eventually released in 2005 and granted Icelandic citizenship. Throughout his chess career, he set many records, including beating two components at a quarter-final and semi-final for the world championship with identical scores.

Fischer died in Iceland in 2008.

Theodore Kaczynski—The Harvard graduate turned unabomber

Jenni Louisch via flickr

Theodore Kaczynski, known by most as the "Unabomber," started out as a child prodigy, receiving his acceptance to Harvard University at the age of 16.

He later went on to earn a doctorate in mathematics from the University of Michigan where his thesis paper was so complex, his professors at the time admitted not really being able to understand it.

At 25, Kaczynski became the youngest professor at the University of California, Berkeley but resigned two years later, moved in with his parents and eventually to a secluded cabin in the woods.

His mail bombing spree lasted twenty years, killed three people and injured 23. He is currently serving a life sentence.

But before the Unabomber, there was a young boy who measured an IQ of 167 in the fifth grade.

Kim Ung-Yong—A guest physics student at age three

Facebook

At the age of three, Kim Ung-Yong began taking courses as a guest physics student at Hanyang University in South Korea. By the age of eight, he was invited by NASA to study in the United States.

Born in 1962, Kim Ung-Yong is listed as having the highest IQ at 210 in the Guinness Book of World Records.

The young prodigy began speaking at four months old and merely two years later, he was able to read in Japanese, Korean, German and English. As a 16-year-old, Kim left NASA and decided to attend college in Korea to earn a doctorate in civil engineering.

Kim has been an adjunct professor at Chungbuk University since 2007 and has published approximately 90 papers on hydraulics in scientific journals.

Sufiah Yusof—The troubled prodigy

bunnyrich via YouTube

In 1997, Sufiah Yusof received her acceptance to St. Hilda's College, Oxford to study mathematics at the age of 13. A few years later, the Malaysian intellect disappeared form her flat after a final examination. She was eventually found working as a waitress in an Internet café and claimed her parent's intense pressure on her to succeed led to the runaway.

Upon her return, Yusof lived with a foster family and gave her undergraduate degree another attempt in 2003. The following year, she married a lawyer from Oxford and never completed her program. The marriage lasted 13 months. In 2007, it was discovered that the once child prodigy has since been working as a prostitute. The news was revealed days after her father was charged with sexually assaulting two 15-year-olds.

Yusof is now reported to be working as a social worker.

Kathleen Holtz—The youngest lawyer

Facebook

Kathleen Holtz started California State University, Los Angeles at the age of ten and graduated magna cum laude with a degree in philosophy. As a 15-year-old, she started law school and became the youngest lawyer in California and, most likely, the nation at the age of 18 in 2007. The average age for individuals taking the bar exam in California is 30.

After passing the bar, Holtz worked for the law firm TroyGould.

In 2009, NBC was reportedly planning a television series based on Holtz' story starring Hilary Duff.

Michael Kearney—The world's youngest university graduate

The Early Show

Kearney on AOL's Gold Rush

At age ten, Michael Kearney received a bachelor's degree from the University of South Alabama and at 17, he received his second graduate degree from Vanderbilt University.

Hawaiian-born, Kearney is listed as the world's youngest university graduate in the Guinness Book of World Records.

At 21, Kearney had collected four undergraduate degrees and a year later, he received his doctorate in chemistry.

In 2006, Kearney won $1 million in AOL's Gold Rush and $25,000 on Who Wants To Be a Millionaire in 2008.

He has had early aspirations to be a game show host. At a young age, Kearney was diagnosed with Attention Deficit Hyperactivity Disorder.

Gregory Smith—The four-time Nobel Peace Prize nominee

University of Virginia

In 1999, at ten years old Gregory Smith received a four-year scholarship to Randolph-Macon College worth approximately $70,000. The young boy eventually graduated cum laude with a Bachelor of Science in Mathematics and minors in History and Biology.

Two years later, Smith added meeting with Bill Clinton and Mikhail Gorbachev, speaking in front of the United Nations, and being nominated for a Nobel Peace Prize to his list of life achievements.

Smith has been nominated for the Nobel Peace Prize three times since then for his humanitarian work in East Timor, Sao Paolo, Rwanda and Kenya.

As a 16-year-old, Smith entered the University of Virginia to study for doctorates in mathematics, aerospace engineering, international relations and biomedical research.

Colin Carlson—The environmentalist boy genius

University of Connecticut

Colin Carlson taught himself how to read as a toddler and graduated from Stanford University Online High School by the age of 11.

At nine-years-old, he began taking college credit courses at the University of Connecticut and enrolled in the university full-time as a sophomore by the age of 12.

Carlson currently holds a 3.9 grade point average as a dual-degree honors student in ecology & evolutionary biology and environmental studies.

He recently filed an age discrimination complaint against the university when they denied his request to participate in field work that would require him to travel to South Africa.

The boy genius has interned with the Sierra Club, founded an environmental organization and testified before the state legislature.

Jacob Barnett—The next Nobel Peace Prize winner

mathboysmom via YouTube

At the age of eight, Jacob Barnett began attending Indiana University-Purdue University Indianapolis (IUPUI).

With an IQ of 170 – higher than Albert Einstein's – Barnett could be in line for a future Nobel Peace Prize, according to one of the world's leading scientists and the 13-year-old's professor at college.

His mother told the Indianapolis Star that her son tested out of algebra 1 and 2, geometry, trigonometry and calculus after two-weeks of studying on the front porch.

Barnett has not let Aspergers Syndrome, a mild form of autism, slow him down.

Since enrollment, Barnett has been taking advanced astrophysics classes and is working on expanding Einstein's theory of relativity. He is also working on challenging the Big Bang theory.

Akrit Jaswal—The seven-year-old surgeon

MohamED88 via flickr

At seven years old, Akrit Jaswal added "surgeon" to his resume.

Born in 1993, the child surgeon became India's youngest physician and university student.

The only downfall is that the young intellect knows just how gifted he is, reportedly saying, "People saw my potential and wanted to help me excel in life...I think they're of above average intelligence, but not as clever as me."

Jaswal has an estimated IQ of 146.

Saffron Pledger – possibly one of the youngest members of a high IQ society

nerissa's ring via flickr

She hasn't even experienced proper schooling yet, but three-year-old Saffron Pledger already has an IQ score of 140 and might possibly become one of the youngest member of Mensa, an intellectual high IQ society with members in more than 100 countries.

In order to be a part of the scholarly society, members must score among the top two percent of the world's IQ scores.

With her current score, Pledger is already 40 points above the national average and three points ahead of former President Bill Clinton.

The English-born Pledger is reported to be able to write, read, count up to 50 and solve simple mathematics.

She is the daughter of eight-time game show champion Danny Pledger, a 23-year-old web designer.

http://www.businessinsider.com/child-prodigies-2011-5?op=1

12

9 Child Prodigies (Who Actually Ended Up Doing Something)

Rick Chillot

The road from kid genius to adult dud is a well-traveled one. But if you or someone you love happens to be a budding brainiac, don't despair. Here are some wonder boys and girls who bucked the trend and grew up to be smart cookies.

1. BLAISE PASCAL (1623-1662)

Areas of Expertise: Math, physical science, and philosophy

Notable Achievement: Making a bet with God

Secret to His Success: Doing geometry when his dad wasn't looking

The great French thinker Blaise Pascal began studying geometry at age 12, even though his father had forbidden such academic endeavors and removed all mathematics textbooks from the house. But even Pascal senior couldn't help but be impressed when his son recreated the geometry theories of Euclid, so he started taking young Poindexter to weekly meetings with the elite mathematicians of Paris. By age 19, Pascal had begun to develop a hand-held, mechanical calculator, which might have made him rich if it hadn't proved impractical to mass produce (a big relief to the abacus industry). Fortunately, that didn't send him spiraling into child-burnout depression, and he went on to many more years of scientific achievement. Besides publishing influential treatises in geometry, Pascal made significant contributions in physical science, like experimenting with atmospheric pressure and determining that a vacuum exists outside Earth's atmosphere. His contributions to philosophy include the famous "Pascal's Wager," which states that believing in God costs you nothing if you're wrong, and wins you everything if you're right.

2. MARIA AGNESI (1718-1799)

Areas of Expertise: Mathematics and astronomy

Notable Achievement: Proving that chicks are good at math, too

Secret to Her Success: Time management; she was known to write the solutions to difficult math problems in her sleep (literally)

When Maria Gaetana Agnesi was born in Milan in 1718, girls in upper-class Italian society were taught dressmaking, etiquette and religion, but not how to read. Thankfully, her father, himself a mathematician, recognized Maria's amazing memory and talent for languages and decided that something like literacy might be a good thing for his daughter. By the time she was nine, Agnesi was impressing party guests with speeches she'd translated into Latin. By age 13, when a visitor would ask her for a waltz, Agnesi would treat her dance partner to a discussion of Newton's theory of gravity (a second waltz was a rare request). But thanks to her father's second and third marriages, Agnesi eventually found herself in charge of a household of 20 brothers and sisters, and since she was the oldest, she ended up utilizing more of those Home Ec skills than she had anticipated. Fortunately, in between breaking up slap fights and doling out bowls of spaghetti, the 30-year-old Agnesi managed to compose a highly influential, two-volume manual on mathematics that included cutting edge developments like integral and differential calculus. Afterward,

Pope Benedict XIV wrote Agnesi, commending her work and suggesting her for a post at the University of Bologna.

3. FELIX MENDELSSOHN (1809-1847)

Areas of Expertise: Piano, organ, and orchestra (performance and composition)

Notable Achievement: His "Wedding March," which has survived over a century of rising divorce rates and overpriced wedding planners

Secret to His Success: Nicest guy in classical music

Widely regarded as the 19th-century equivalent of Mozart, German composer Felix Mendelssohn was musically precocious at an early age. Mendelssohn began taking piano lessons at age six, made his first public performance at age nine, and wrote his first composition (that we know of) when he was 11. By the time he turned 17, he had completed his Overture to "A Midsummer Night's Dream," one of the Romantic period's best-known, most-loved works of classical music. Then, in 1835, Mendelssohn's father died, which (just like Wolfy) came as a crushing blow to the composer. But rather than sending him into an alcohol-induced stupor, the experience motivated Felix to finish his oratorio, "St. Paul," which had been one of his father's dying requests. From there, he went on to compose important and popular works, including the "Wedding March." In 1843, at age 34, Mendelssohn founded the Conservatory of Music in Leipzig, where he taught composition with fellow musical great Robert Schumann.

4. MARIE CURIE (1867-1934)

Areas of Expertise: Physics, chemistry and radioactivity

Notable Achievement: The first woman to win a Nobel Prize ; and just for good measure, she won two

Secret to Her Success: Wanted to be in her element, so she discovered it

Born in Warsaw, Poland, Marie Sklodowska was the child of two teachers who placed great importance on education for all of their children. This wasn't a problem for four-year-old Marie, who, just by hanging around her four older siblings, taught herself how to read (Russian and French) and was known to help her brothers and sisters with their math homework. It was also at age four that she began to freak people out with her incredible memory, as she was able to recall events that had happened years before ("Remember that time when I was three months old and you put my diaper on backwards, idiot?"⊠) As a teenager, Marie was anxious to attend college, but her family couldn't afford it since her father had lost his teaching job, so she spent five grueling years earning money as a governess (it wasn't like The Sound of Music at all; the kids were stupid, and there was no singing or dancing). But her time came in 1891, and she headed for the Sorbonne in Paris. There, she discovered future husband Pierre Curie, along with the radioactive elements radium and polonium. In her thirties, Marie worked closely with her husband, and together they devised the science of radioactivity, for which they were awarded a Nobel Prize in physics. After Pierre's death in 1906, Marie continued her work, winning her second Nobel (this time in chemistry) at age 44.

5. PABLO PICASSO (1881-1973)

Areas of Expertise: Painting, drawing, sculpture

Notable Achievement: The most famous name in modern art

Secret to His Success: Quantity and quality

Everyone knows that Picasso achieved artistic fame and success as an adult, but little Pablo was quite the prodigy, too. In fact, it's said that Picasso had an interest in drawing even before he could speak. Perhaps that's why, once he finally could talk, he immediately started demanding that his father (an artist himself) give him his paintbrushes. And when he became old enough to go to school, pushy little Pablo said he would only go on the condition that, while there, he could draw as much as he liked. Fortunately, the headmaster and the other students recognized Picasso's gift, and more or less allowed him to come, go, and work as he pleased. Years later, the adult Picasso attended an exhibit of children's drawings and commented that he could never have been in such a show because at age 12, he "drew like Raphael."☒ A little modesty might have done him some good, but in fact, drawings that survive from his childhood suggest that prepubescent Pablo could indeed have given the great Renaissance artist a run for his money . Picasso's many contributions to modern art—including cubism, "Guernica,"☒ and people drawn with two eyes on one side of their face—are too exhaustive to list here. By the time of his death, he'd created over 22,000 works of art.

6. JEAN PIAGET (1896-1980)

Area of Expertise: Child psychology

Notable Achievement: Changing the way we think about the way children think

Secret to His Success: The ability to hold conversations with three-year-olds

Does it take a child who's interested in psychology to make a child psychologist? Apparently not. When Jean Piaget was growing up in Neuchâtel, Switzerland, his area of expertise was zoology. He talked his way into a job at the local Museum of Natural History at the age of 10, where he developed a keen interest in mollusks (especially snails). By high school, he'd published so many papers on the subject that his name was well known among European mollusk experts (most of whom assumed he was an adult). So later in life, when his interests turned to psychology, Piaget's zoological background led him to seek out the "biological explanation of knowledge."⊠ Suspecting that observing children might lead to an answer, he came up with an earth-shattering new way to explore how children think: by watching them, listening to them, and talking to them. Piaget deduced that a child's mind isn't a blank slate, but is constantly imagining and testing new theories about the world and how it works. This revelation, plus his 75 years of scientific research, spawned whole new fields of psychology. He might even have had an explanation for why your kid put that peanut butter-and-jelly sandwich in the VCR.

7. JASCHA HEIFETZ (1901-1987)

Area of Expertise: Violin maestro

Notable Achievement: Setting the standard for 20th-century violinists

Secret to His Success: When he played the violin, it made his teachers cry (in a good way)

Little Jascha's interest in music was noticeable at only eight months of age, when he reportedly smiled at his father's violin playing, but winced in pain whenever Dad hit the wrong note. When Jascha turned three, he asked for—and received—his first violin and promptly started taking lessons. So naturally, Heifetz was giving public concerts by the age of five (about the same time the rest of us started eating paste). At age 16, Jascha's family moved to the United States to dodge the Russian Revolution, and before long, he had his debut at Carnegie Hall, where he wowed critics and became an overnight musical idol.

Musical burn-out seemed almost inevitable, but Heifetz continued touring into his sixties and kept recording into his seventies (take that, Keith Richards), racking up Grammy after Grammy without releasing a single music video. Heifetz once called being a child prodigy "a disease which is generally fatal," and one that he "was among the few to have good fortune to survive."

8. JOHN VON NEUMANN (1903-1957)

Areas of Expertise: Quantum mechanics, information theory, computer science

Notable Achievements: Developing the hydrogen bomb and a few early computers

Secret to His Success: Not too bookish to enjoy a good kegger

As a child in Budapest, Hungary, JÃ¡nos von Neumann amazed adults and annoyed fellow six-year olds by dividing eight-digit numbers in his head, speaking in Greek, and memorizing pages out of the phone book. He published his first scientific paper while still a teenager, but because of Hungary's rising anti-Semitic atmosphere, he decided to pursue his mathematics career elsewhere. Unfortunately, he chose to go to Germany, which clearly didn't turn out to be such a hot idea. After he was offered a position at Princeton University, von Neumann headed to the States, choosing to adopt the first name John. In America, he was free to hang around with other expatriate eggheads, including future magazine cover model Albert Einstein. In between throwing raucous parties, ogling secretaries, and getting into car accidents (he was a notoriously reckless driver), von Neumann worked on theoretical mathematics and various real-world projects, including the development of the hydrogen bomb and construction of one of the first working computers.

9. PAUL ERDÖS (1913-1996)

Area of Expertise: Mathematics

Notable Achievements: It would take a mathematician to explain them

Secret to His Success: Loved numbers, tolerated everything else

Paul Erdös was multiplying three-digit numbers for kicks when he was three. At age four, he started playing around with prime and negative numbers. Not much later, he developed a cute little habit of asking people their ages and then computing how many seconds they'd been alive. Never able to shake his passion for numbers, Erdös grew up to become arguably the most prolific mathematician in history, authoring or co-authoring almost 1,500 mathematical papers. In fact, collaborating with Erdös was such a point of prestige that—to this day—to this day—mathematicians assign themselves "Erdös numbers," which works sort of like the fabled Kevin Bacon game. An Erdös number indicates how closely a person has worked with the great one: Those who co-authored a paper with him have a number of 1, those who wrote a paper with one of his co-authors have a number of 2, and so on. Never had the pleasure of writing a mathematics paper? Congratulations , you have an Erdös number of infinity. Now go balance your checkbook.

13

THE DOWNSIDE OF BEING
A CHILD PRODIGY

Philippe M. Frowd

Alissa Quart learned to read at three. By the time she was five, her father counted on her to offer presentations on modernist art. In elementary school, she taught her own friends to read. By seven, she had written her first novel; at 10, she was lecturing her companions on everything from film stock to astrology. She routinely read a book a day. When she was a 13-year-old high school freshman, she edited her father's writing. By 17, she had won a dozen creative-writing competitions.

A dream childhood that would handily prepare a bright youngster for the intellectual rigors of life, right? Not really, writes Quart, now 34, in her new book, Hothouse Kids: The Dilemma of the Gifted Child (Penguin Press). "Having been built in the fashion I was as a child — created and then deflated — has left me with a distinct feeling of failure." Quart is unflinchingly honest about her unusual childhood experience. "My father would have bristled at the notion that he was an overbearing puppet master. If I sat absolutely quietly and wrote lyrical verse about tree-tops, I was peachy. My father was hell-bent on bettering my lot — and by extension our family's lot." But, continues Quart in Hothouse Kids, "I was far too young for the Czech films and the difficult novels I was coerced to digest. My father's plan succeeded on one level, of course. I became a hothouse kid."

In her book, Quart explores the pressures that are brought to bear on those children designated gifted or prodigies. True prodigies are very rare, says Quart. Her definition of prodigy: "a child with a skill set or an ability that is incredibly accomplished, far beyond their years." They tend to be in chess, music and math, more in quantitative fields and less in qualitative disciplines, where "kids are gifted in ways that are hard to measure." But then there is Marla Olmstead, a four-year-old artist whom Quart visited, whose dozens of brightly colored abstract oil paintings have brought in $300,000, as well as calls from Oprah and David Letterman. Some prodigies make successful transitions to adult accomplishment, but others flounder as they get older. Gifted children, an intellectual step down from prodigyhood, tend to be identified with high IQ scores. (Quart is quick to say that she herself was not a prodigy.)

In a culture of ambitious parenting that has yielded prenatal child enrichment products (e.g., BabyPlus Womb Songs) and high-concept teaching devices (Baby Einstein DVDs), parents feel an increasing amount of anxiety about helping their offspring keep up with the neighbors' kids. But such measures don't necessarily work, writes Quart, and may even backfire. "Designating children as gifted, especially extremely gifted, and cultivating that giftedness may be not only a waste of money , but positively harmful," she writes. "The overcultivated can develop self-esteem problems and performance anxiety." An extreme example was Brandenn Bremmer, a teenager with an IQ over 160, who made national news when he entered college at age 10. He told Quart in an interview, "America is a society that demands perfection."In March 2005, at the age of 14, he committed suicide by shooting himself in the head.

These issues are not abstractions to Quart, who told TIME that she is still struggling with them. "I just got married, and I'm trying to figure that out how to parent. Children who are told that they're gifted, talented or special may well not perform or feel as good as a child who's merely told, you've done a job nicely, you did it well, I'm so glad you did it like that, you're doing great." Her advice to others? "Emphasize the work in itself, the process itself, the activity. The kids are trying, they're doing a good job, they're learning how to do something. Each thing they do is discrete; it's not part of a larger identity of being spectacular."

Quart sought out former prodigies and gifted kids while researching her book, as well as the parents of high-achieving children. Her hard work has paid off: her book has garnered praise from such publications as Publishers Weekly: "Quart's second book is first-class literary journalism." Mary Pipher, the best-selling author of Reviving Ophelia, is also a fan: "[Quart's] conclusions manage to be both commonsensical and profound. In the end, she makes a scholarly argument for the benefits of sandboxes, recess and goofing off. I love this woman." And many parents might too, if they can benefit from Quart's hard-earned wisdom about how to nurture talent gently, without crushing it.

http://content.time.com/time/arts/
article/0,8599,1532087,00.html#ixzz2qqrbgEWi

14

FAMILY UNDER THE MICROSCOPE

Oliver James

Child prodigies are made not born –
and later on don't always shine

In general, you are more likely to pursue a similar profession to one of your parents and if you are a prodigy, the field is almost always one in which your parents were accomplished, or wished that they had been. Such children are hothoused through regimes of accelerated learning. A typical example is John Adams, who passed O-levels when he was eight and A-levels a year later.

His father, Ken, published a book (sanguinely entitled – as his son was a prodigy, not a genius – Your Child Can Be A Genius) giving a detailed account of the fanatical parenting by which this was achieved. There are numerous mathematical prodigies whose parents even went so far as to move with their prepubescent child to a university town so that the studies could be pursued at a higher level.

Although outstanding early ability tends to be presented in the media as a genetic freak, this is probably almost never the case, except perhaps in a handful of isolated skills, such as being able to calculate (there are children who for no apparent external, nurtured reason are able to multiply and divide improbably difficult numbers without blinking). There are virtually no authenticated cases of prodigies who have come from families in which they were not hothoused or otherwise helped.

In the early years, the parents go to tremendous lengths to make it abundantly clear that love is conditional on the acquisition of particular skills. Subsequently, no expense is spared to obtain the best possible teaching. Nearly all prodigious modern sportsmen and women, such as the tennis players Venus and Serena Williams, have been obsessively coached from a young age, usually with their parents watching from the sidelines. In the case of the Williams sisters, their father declared his intention of creating world-beaters from the moment of their birth.

Yet childhood prodigy is far from necessarily the precursor of adult genius; in the vast majority of cases it is not. Nor is it about being clever. High marks in intelligence tests do not guarantee lifetime achievement. A famous study of 400 American children with IQs above 140 (the average is 100) found that they did nothing special in later life for people of their social class. None of them became geniuses and if anything, the capacity to pass exams or do well at IQ tests may be more a measure of your desire to please parents and teachers than of originality.

When I used to administer IQ tests to children while working as a child psychologist, there was a question along the lines of "You are playing with a ball and another child comes and takes it away. What do you do?" Even as young as five, the "clever" children would be all set to say "thump him" before fixing me with a beady eye. Thinking, "he obviously doesn't want the true answer, so what's he got in mind?" they would say "I'd tell the teacher."

The less people-pleasing ones would get no marks for not worrying what I wanted to hear, but it is often from their ranks that truly original creators come. In the field of entrepreneurial business high-achievers, for example, a high proportion do not even obtain GCSEs. People-pleasing and breaking moulds do not go together.

When it comes to achievement, motivation is hugely important. While politicians bang on about "ability" and "talent" as if it is "God-given" (as Tony Blair once put it), these come out of relationships with parents and a consequent desire to succeed, much more so than genes.

Prodigies early years: Howe, MJA, 2007, in Ciba Foundation Symposium 178 – The Origin and Development of High Ability, eds Bock, GR et al, Novartis. More Oliver James at selfishcapitalist.com

http://www.theguardian.com/lifeandstyle/2009/oct/17/ oliver-james-child-prodigies

15

When Does Nurturing a Gifted Child Become Pushing?

Carol Bainbridge

Parents are rightfully proud of their child's abilities and talents. They are also right to provide opportunities that will nurture those abilities and talents. But when does nurturing become pushing?

A simple way to answer that question is to consider the difference between nurturing and pushing. Basically, nurturing is child-centered, while pushing is adult-centered. When we nurture we follow the child's lead, but when we push, we want the child to follow us, to do what we want him or her to do. If the difference is so simple, why do so many parents continue to wonder whether they are pushing their children?

To understand why is is hard to distinguish between the nurturing and pushing, consider the following situation:

A mother takes Jimmy, her two-year-old, to visit a friend, who has a piano in the living room. As toddlers do, Jimmy explores the room and eventually finds the piano, touching the keys and noticing that touching different keys results in different sounds. He can't seem to get enough of the piano.

From that day on, whenever Jimmy visits a home with a piano, he makes a bee line for it and begins to play with the keys. If he sees keyboards in a toy store, he wants to go up to them and play them. Jimmy clearly has an unusual interest in pianos; most children don't behave this way. Because Jimmy's mother wants to nurture his interests, she buys him a keyboard. By the time Jimmy is four years old, his mother has decided he should have piano lessons since he plays with his keyboard frequently and can play some simple songs and even tries to make up some songs.

Is buying a keyboard for a two-year-old pushing? Is arranging lessons for a four-year-old pushing?

Most of us would probably say, "no." In neither case is Jimmy's mom pushing him. Jimmy is clearly interested and his mother is trying to provide opportunities to foster that interest.

Now go one step farther. Once Jimmy has piano lessons , he doesn't always want to practice scales. He still enjoys playing his keyboard, but he doesn't want to practice the scales or the songs his teacher has assigned, songs that will help him develop his skills. Jimmy's mother insists that Jimmy practice the required thirty minutes a day and will sometimes take away some of Jimmy's privileges because he won't practice.

Is insisting on thirty minutes practice every day pushing?

Some parents will say, "no," because practicing scales is not especially interesting, but it is necessary. Other parents will say, "yes," it is pushing because now the piano playing is adult-centered, not child-centered. It is Jimmy's mother who insists that Jimmy practice that leads to Jimmy practicing. Jimmy is no longer playing on his own.

Take yet another step in the story of Jimmy and his interest in piano playing. Imagine now that Jimmy's mother notices that after practicing thirty minutes almost every day, Jimmy's piano playing has increased tremendously. In fact, his teacher has commented that she has never seen a child so young with so much talent. Now Jimmy's mother insists that Jimmy practice an hour every day, but soon that becomes two hours every day. Jimmy is not allowed to play ball games for fear that he will hurt his fingers. Jimmy has other interests, but his mother insists that he focus on piano playing. She envisions Jimmy as a famous piano prodigy or at least a famous pianist as an adult. Is this pushing?

With the latest move, Jimmy's mother has moved from nurturing to pushing Jimmy. Insisting that Jimmy practice scales and songs he's not interested in for a recommended thirty minutes a day is not pushing. Gifted children resist what they consider boring activities, even in areas of their interest.

Jimmy's mother knows, however, that unless Jimmy learns the scales, he won't develop the skills he needs to play the piano the way he seems to want to.

However, thirty minutes a day is not excessive and it doesn't interfere with his other interests and activities. When Jimmy's mother insists he practice two hours a day and prevents him from engaging in other activities, she is pushing him. She has also gotten caught up in her son's potential future as a pianist and is letting that, rather than her son's interest, guide her. That is clearly pushing.

What about other abilities? When does nurturing become pushing?

The same basic principle applies regardless of the skill or ability a gifted child exhibits. A parent who notices that his or her child is showing early signs of reading may want to "test" the child. For example, a preschooler may see a word in a book or on a billboard and say the word. Did the child really "read" that word? It's natural for a parent to test that. The parent might show the child another word and ask what the word is.

This kind of testing is not pushing. If the child seems to enjoy the guessing game, a parent might go a step farther and buy flash cards. If a child is not interested, and a parent buys flashcards and insists that the child work with them because the parent believes the child's future will be brighter if the child learns to read early, then the parent is pushing. However, as long as the child enjoys the activity, it is not pushing.

Parents of gifted children often find that they cannot provide enough information, cannot teach their children enough. In fact, many parents of gifted children scoff at the idea that they are pushing their children. They complain that their children are dragging them along.

The Boundary Between Nurturing and Pushing

These examples help illustrate the difference between nurturing and pushing, between child-centered and adult-centered learning. All parents know that there will be times their children will not want to do what they are supposed to do, to learn what they are supposed to learn. Gifted children may be smart, but they are still children and don't always know what is best for them. Little Jimmy knew he wanted to play the piano, but he didn't understand the need to practice what he considered boring scales.

Certainly, then, times will arise when parents do have to nudge their children, but when the parents' interests rather than the child's interests determine what is learned, then it becomes pushing.

http://giftedkids.about.com/od/nurturinggiftsandtalents/qt/pushing.htm

16

Top 5 Ways to Nurture Gifted Children

Carol Bainbridge

"Is my child gifted?" That is the question asked most often by parents of gifted children. After that question, the most frequently asked question is "How do I nurture my gifted child?" Here are five simple answers to that question.

1. Follow Your Child's Lead

What does your child enjoy? What does your child seem to be good at? Provide opportunities for your child to works with things he or she enjoys or is good at. For example, if your child loves dinosaurs, get books about dinosaurs, fiction and non-fiction. Get games and puzzles about dinosaurs. Go see dinosaurs at museums. If your child is good at music or a sport, provide opportunities for him or her to learn an instrument or play a sport.

2. Expand Your Child's Interests

While it's important to provide opportunities for your child to work with his or her interests and strengths, it is also important to expose your child to new things. Children only know what they have been exposed to, so if they've never been exposed to music, they may not know whether they like it or are good at it. Children need not be forced to try new things, but they should be encouraged. It is not forcing a child, however, to insist that they not quit something after two days.

3. Be Creative

This may seem as though it's easier said than done, but once you start thinking "outside the box," it gets easier. Gifted children love to think and solve problems, so provide them with ample opportunities for doing so. For example, if your preschooler or kindergartner likes to read, you might write daily notes to pack in their lunch box. If your child likes science, you might cook together and then ask your child why vegetables get soft when they're cooked or why cakes rise when they're baked.

4. Look for Outside Activities

Many towns offer classes for children as do museums, zoos, community theaters, and many universities and community colleges . In addition, most every region has places of historical interest. Some also have botanical gardens, planetariums, and other places of interest. If you are unsure of what is available in your area, you can call or visit the nearest "welcome center" for your state or province. They have this kind of information to give to visitors.

5. Keep a Variety of Resources at Home

These resources need not be expensive or elaborate. They just need to allow your gifted child to develop his or her interests or get exposed to new ones. For example, to encourage artistic talent, all you need initially are simple paint brushes and a paint box, plain white paper, crayons, and other basic supplies. It's not difficult to create boxes of such materials for your child to use whenever he or she is interested.

http://giftedkids.about.com/od/nurturinggiftsandtalents/tp/ simplenurture.htm

17

WHAT IS A GIFTED CHILD?

Carol Bainbridge

Gifted or not gifted? Is everyone gifted? Is no one gifted? What does a gifted child look like? These are questions that are asked frequently by parents and others. Describing a gifted child is difficult because not everyone defines "gifted" the same way. As difficult as it is, it is still possible to provide a general description of typical gifted children because they have many similar traits. The more you learn about gifted children, the easier it becomes to identify them.

High IQ:

• Mildly Gifted -- 115 to 129

• Moderately Gifted -- 130 to 144

• Highly Gifted -- 145 to 159

• Exceptionally Gifted -- 160 to 179

• Profoundly Gifted -- 180

These ranges are based on a standard bell curve. Most people fall in the range between 85 and 115, with 100 the absolute norm. This range is considered normal. The farther away from the absolute norm of 100 a child is, the greater the need for special educational accommodations, regardless of whether the distance is on the left or right of 100.

Exceptional Talent:

Exceptional talent is the ability to perform a skill at a level usually not reached until later years, sometimes as late as adulthood. A three-year old may be reading like a third grader or a nine-year-old may be playing piano like an 18 year old, who has studied for years. If the exceptional talent is in a non-academic area such as music or art, the children may not be identified as gifted by the school because most testing for gifted programs is based on academic ability or achievement.

High Achievement:

Gifted children are usually, but not always, high achievers. Even when they don't achieve good grades, they tend to score high on achievement tests, most often in the 95-99 percentile range. They love to learn and their love of learning, good memories, and ability to learn quickly and easily enable them to succeed. However, if a gifted child has lost the motivation to learn, he or she may not do well in school, although achievement test scores will usually remain high.

Potential to Achieve or Excel:

Whether or not a gifted child excels in school, he or she has the potential to do so. Many gifted children are intrinsically motivated, which means the motivation comes from within. They become motivated by interest and challenge. When these children are interested and appropriately challenged, they can and will achieve. However, even though a gifted child may not be achieving in school, he or she may still be learning and achieving on their own at home.

Heightened Sensitivity:

Although heightened sensitivity is rarely, if ever, used to identify gifted children in school, it is so common among gifted children that it is one of the characteristics that set them apart from other children. They may be emotionally sensitive, crying over what others considered trivial. They may be physically sensitive, bothered by tags on shirts or seams on socks. Psychologist Kazimierz Dabrowski called these "over-excitabilities."

http://giftedkids.about.com/od/gifted101/p/gifteddef.htm

18

DOES WRITING PRODIGY EXIST? HOW TO IDENTIFY AND NURTURE CHILDREN WITH EXTRAORDINARY WRITING TALENT

Jane Piirto

Talent Development: Proceedings from The 1991 Henry B. and Jocelyn Wallace National Research Symposium on Talent Development, pp.387-388

This article is a book chapter excerpted from Talent Development. Author Jane Piirto states that writing prodigy may in fact be more common than previously thought. She provides an example and identifies 16 characteristics found in students who are writing at an advanced level of competence.

Abstract

Writing prodigy may occur more frequently than commonly thought. Little analytical work has been done on the quality of the writing of young gifted children. The writing of seven students was analyzed: (1) four were selected from 400 students from a Manhattan, New York City, school for gifted children where mean IQ is 140+; (2) three were brought to the attention of the author by professional writers, parents, and administrators. Sixteen characteristics that determine the quality of the writing of talented young writers were generated. Biographies of adult creative writers were studied to determine situational factors that may lead to adult creative production in writing. This presentation is based on a chapter in a book: (Piirto, J. [in press].Understanding those who create. Dayton, OH: Ohio Psychology Press).

Summary:

The studies of adult creative writers have shown that they were early and passionate readers, encountering the written word with intense enjoyment, often using reading as an escape from the world. Little work has been done on the juvenilia of eminent writers. In fact, little work has been done on the quality of youthful creative production in most of the arts. Feldman (1986), in Nature's Gambit, did six case studies, and used the common definition that a prodigy is generally understood as being a child aged ten or under who produces work that is similar to that of adult professionals. Radford (1990), in Child Prodigies And Exceptional Early Achievers said that prodigies may also be older than ten, and their achievements may not have to have "lasting merit" (p.40). Feldman studied one writing prodigy and he asserted that prodigies are not commonly found in the writing domain. He gave two reasons: "The field itself has few organized supports or strategies for instruction in the craft..,(and) children normally lack the kind of experience, insight, and understanding that writers are expected to convey in their works" (p. 44).

There do seem to exist some children who do produce work in writing on an adult level of competence (Piirto, 1987, 1989a. b). I have studied the work of seven children. Here is an example of extraordinary poetry written by a child.

Sweet aromas fill the stallion's heart

Eyes of blue, hide of white,

Glimmering with its sweat

On the run, under burning sun.

As quick as a shimmering, sunny stream.

Panting wildly, wildly panting

Suede rabbit hops in its way.

This is a poem by a 9 year old girl. It illustrates unusual linguistic precocity in the repetition of consonant and vowel sounds (assonance and consonance), the sophisticated rhythms ("Eyes of blue, hide of white"; "on the run, under burning sun"; "Panting wildly, wildly panting") and the improbable images ("suede"). This girl was enrolled in a school for intellectually gifted children, but her ability far surpassed those of her intellectually gifted peers. A letter from her mother in 1990 said that she has continued to write and is in high school now, writing novels.

"Sweet aromas" in the horse's heart creates an initial paradox. It is not known, nor is it logical, that there would be aromas in a horse's heart. This girl pays no attention to the logic. The second line uses the repetitive device of parallel structure to create a rhythm. The third line sets ups visual image that is answered in line five--"glimmering" and "shimmering." In the fourth line, the letters "r", "u", and "n", are repeated in various melodic combinations: "run", "under", "burning," and then, the "run" is resolved into "sun," which is repeated in the next line, in an alliterative phrase, "shimmering sunny stream." The urgency of the reversed phrases in the fifth line, "panting wildly, wildly panting," keeps the excitement of the poem. Then, when a "suede" rabbit hops, we can feel the danger inherent in that ordinary situation. The use of the unusual adjective, "suede," to describes rabbit is in no way the usual cliche that people come up with when they refer to rabbits.

These are some of the qualities found in the writing of such children: (a) the use of paradox; (b) the use of parallel structure; (c) the use of rhythm; (d) the use of visual imagery; (e) melodic combinations; (f) unusual use of figures of speech, e.g.. alliteration, personification, and assonance; (g) confidence with reverse structure; (h) unusual adjectives and adverbs; (i) a feeling of movement; (j) uncanny wisdom; (k) sophisticated syntax using punctuation marks such as hyphens, parentheses, and semi-colons; (I) prose lyricism; (m) display of a "natural ear" for language; (n) sense of humor; (o) philosophical or moral bent; and (p) a willingness to "play" with words.

The early lives of such writers as George Eliot, Stephen Crane, Jane Austen, Sinclair Lewis, Dylan Thomas, Virginia Woolf, the Bronte sisters and brother, Tennessee Williams, John Updike, and Harry Crews are illustrative that many prominent writers wrote and read young, engaging the written word with commitment, emotion, imagination, and intellectual excitement. These experiences enabled the writers to achieve automaticity.

References

Feldman, D. (1986). Nature's gambit: Child prodigies and the development of human potential. New York Basic.

Piirto, J. (1987). The existence of writing prodigy. Paper presented at the National Association for Gifted Children Conference. New Orleans.

Piirto, J. (1989a). Does writing prodigy exist? Creativity Research Journal, 2. 134-135.

Piirto. J. (1988, May/June). Linguistic prodigy: Does it exist? Gifted Children Monthly, pp. 1-2.

Piirto, J. (in press). Creativity and giftedness. Dayton, OH: Ohio Psychology Press.

Radford, J. (1990). Child prodigies and exceptional early achievers. New York: Macmillan/The Free Press.

http://www.davidsongifted.org/db/Articles_id_10010.aspx

19

ATTENTION TRAINING

Joseph Cardillo

Gifted Children: Nurturing Genius (Part One)

Nurturing gifted children.

"Beethoven had a music teacher who described him as *hopeless*." [Likewise] Picasso was so disinterested in school when he was a young boy that the only way his family could get him to go was by letting him bring a live chicken to class so he could draw its portrait," (Judy Galbraith, The GiftedKids' Survival Guide). Similarly, Einstein quit high school at the age of 15—dismayed.

"What's up with that?" you might ask.

Dr. Dudley Herschbach of the Department of Chemistry and Chemical Biology, Harvard University who discusses the young Einstein in a paper titled Einstein as a Studentwrites: "Late in life, when reflecting on his uncanny papers of 1905, Einstein liked to say, "Nobody expected me to lay golden eggs." A century later, nobody can expect to fully comprehend how he did it."

Yet, for as much as the world has benefited from the contributions of gifted individuals, it is disturbing, to this writer, to realize that the population least likely to learn and achieve its potential is the highly gifted.

Statistics show that 85% of public school educators agree that more needs to be done for gifted students. And many are doing the best job possible given the hand they've been dealt. So one might wonder, why then aren't they—teachers, students, parents, communities—getting the support we need?

In my following series of posts on Gifted Children, I will discuss why these children are likely to fall between the cracks from early on and why they experience the greatest discrepancies between their abilities and what they are generally being asked to do, in particular—but not limited to—academic environments.

Jan and Bob Davidson—founders of the Davidson Institute for Talent Development and authors of the book Genius Denied: How to Stop Wasting Our Brightest Young Minds, What You and Your School Can do for Your Gifted Child, write that genius has two different but interrelated meanings. "In one sense, genius means high intellectual potential; in another sense, genius means creative ability of exceptional high order as demonstrated by total achievement." And they use both.

As such, Davidson programs for the gifted serve what they refer to asprofoundly gifted youth. They define that with tests that are 99.9% or higher or children that are 3 standard deviations above the norm. Depending on the IQ test, children participating in Davidson programs may norm differently and can peak anywhere from 145 to 150 in terms of IQ. The problem, as addressed in Genius Denied, is that "while children of IQs of 120 to 160 may be called gifted, they learn at different rates and think at very different levels." The range "includes students who may be satisfied with moderate academic advancement such as taking algebra in 8th Grade, and more intellectually advanced students who may be ready for calculus in elementary school. It covers students who read just a little above grade level to twelve-year-olds who read Tolstoy by flashlight under the covers at night. Yet educational policies tend to view the gifted as a homogenous group and assume that any gifted program in place will satisfy all these children's needs."

Most schools, public and private, do well providing students with a solid educational foundation. And we have taken some very productive steps in meeting the needs of low-achievers, middle-achievers, and even high-achievers. All kids deserve this.

It seems discriminatory to exclude anyone, regardless of his or her level of achievement—including the profoundly gifted. Unfortunately, it is easy to write them off—thinking they are getting straight A+s. They seem to be doing pretty well for themselves. What more can they possibly need?   My state, New York, for example, currently requires identification of gifted children, but doesn't mandate special programming. What's more,funding in just the past few years has dropped from (a modest) 15 million dollars to zero.

It seems unreasonable to expect to reap the benefits of gifted childrens' contributions if we don't nurture their minds along the way.

In many states, instruction for the gifted must be supplemental to regular instruction. This means in content and in cost. The Davidson's write, "Classes [in such states]that gifted students need most—accelerated math, English, and science—aren't supplementary; they're substitutes for the core curriculum, and therefore they are excluded from gifted programs and so [in such states] many schools that want to do something for gifted students wind up offering them the equivalent of indoor camp."

Picture this: A profoundly gifted young boy, age 9, was enrolled in such a school. His parent explains, they live "in a state that has no mandate to identify or serve gifted children and there is no federal mandate for giftededucation, [and so he was] offered no services whatsoever other than the regular classroom with his age peers where the main concern was "No Child Left Behind." This parent's story is all too common. The parent explains that giftedness in their neck of the woods "is determined by achievement and class engagement in the regular classroom [and since] teachers here are not required to have any training whatsoever in gifted education it is no wonder that this child did not thrive in a regular classroom, and in fact felt extremely isolated, alone and disengaged." This disengagement is a big flag and can lead to other more serious problems.

Another child is growing up in a state that does mandate schools to identify gifted children and to serve them with special educational programs. However, the state (like mine) has no funds allotted for gifted programming. The child, prior to preschool, was, as her parents describe, "lit." In fact, the child has been entertainingly and intelligently curious to her parents since birth. "From the moment she opened her eyes," I could tell there was something different about her," says her mother—a professor. "She has always loved language and could speak very, very early on. When all the parenting books gave a dipstick of about 60 words —she could wield complex sentences easily and at will. Mom recalls how at the age of two, her daughter described a series of gallery of paintings, using language that was elevated enough for the museum's director who overheard to comment on her verbal skill. Her love for language and skill were so out of the norm that mom and dad—educators both—decided, upon a friend's recommendation (an educator of gifted children), to have their daughter tested. When these parents told their pediatrician, he chuckled and commented, "Top 1 %. Right?" The parents were gratefulfor his response because there had been so few others with whom they could share their joys and concerns—as well as their difficult challenges. The pediatrician was pretty much dead on: the child's verbal skills landed her above 99%. Interestingly, the mother recalls, he (the pediatrician) had noticed her daughter's aptitude for communication at 4 months old during a routine appointment, commenting on how—even then— she knew when and where to make baby sounds within a conversation with her mother.

In another story, the parents of a child who at age 3 ½ is measuringkitchen cabinets with a tape-measure (and doing the math) are told by his pre-school teacher, "that sounds a little inflated."

And another profoundly gifted child is being mocked by her classmates and so she is now slowly "phasing out" —insofar as the classroom is concerned—wishing on a daily basis for someone to understand.

What can we do, writes Dr. James R. Delisle, author of the Gifted Kids Survival Book, to "transform genius denied into genius fulfilled?"

To help gather information regarding some commonly shared questions posed by parents and teachers of highly gifted youth, I recently interviewed Jill Adrian, Director of Family Services at the Davidson Institute. The next sequence of posts will present highlights from our discussion and will include commentary on:

· the 1st signs of giftedness

· how parents can mentor their gifted child before pre-school

· things parents can do to advocate once their gifted child enters the system

· cost-effective ways to meet gifted children's needs in schools

· researched guides for deciding on acceleration or not

· what happens if you are met with resistance

· and how to make public education work for you

You will find links to most of these talking points and, especially if you are a parent of a highly gifted child, discover a path and some camaraderie with which to break the silence about what you know already are some very special needs and concerns. With any luck, this series of posts can help provide a little light at the beginning of this proverbial tunnel.

Stay tuned!

"It is almost a miracle that modern teaching methods have not yet entirely strangled the holy curiosity of inquiry; for what

this delicate little plant needs more than anything, besides stimulation, is freedom." – Albert Einstein

http://www.psychologytoday.com/blog/attention-training/201007/gifted-children-nurturing-genius-part-one

20

GIFTED CHILDREN: NURTURING GENIUS (PART TWO)

Joseph Cardillo, Ph.D. in Attention Training

Turning genius denied into genius fulfilled.

Realizing your child is gifted or profoundly gifted, it is not always easy to engage in conversations with people about what to do next. Suffice to say the reasons are many. Similarly it may be difficult to get reliable information that can help guide you, in a timely way, as you must sometimes make important, on-the-fly decisions regarding your child's development, not to mention, draw conclusions and take actions that will help sketch your child's future—as well as yours.

I mentioned in my first post, Gifted Children: Squandering Genius (Part One) that "statistics show that 85% of public school educators already agree that more needs to be done for gifted students. And many are doing the best job possible given the circumstances.

But nonetheless, for as much as the world has benefited from the contributions of gifted individuals, it is disturbing to realize that the population least likely to learn and achieve its potential is the highly gifted.

In an effort to assist parents, teachers, and particularly these uniquely talented children, I have attempted to composite enough information in this article to get us all going.

To this end, I recently spoke with Jill Adrian, Director of Family Services at the Davidson Institute.

A bit of background from the Davidson website: The Davidson Institute, formed in 1999, is a private operating foundation funded by Bob and Jan Davidson to serve profoundly gifted young people under the age of 18. Profoundly gifted students are those who score in the 99,9 percentile on IQ and achievement tests. These students often share the following characteristics:

1. An extreme need for constant mental stimulation

2. An ability to learn and process complex information rapidly

3. A need to explore subjects in surprising depth

4. An insatiable curiosity; endless questions and inquiries

5. A need for precision in thinking and expression-often answering questions with "that depends..."

6. An ability to focus intently on a subject of interest for long periods of time

7. An inability to concentrate on a task that is not intellectually challenging, including repetitious ideas or material presented in small pieces

The Institute also provides information and educational opportunities for teachers, school administrators, school counselors, pediatricians, psychologists, psychiatrists and other professionals.

Sharing ITS gifts from coast-to-coast, the Davidson Institute provides a wide and impressive range of programs: the Davidson Young Scholars Program offers free consulting services for the profoundly gifted from ages 5 – 18; the Davidson Fellows program awards $50,000, $25,000 and $10,000 scholarships in Mathematics, Science, Literature, Music, Technology, Philosophy and Outside the Box; The Davidson Academy a free public school (housed at the University of Nevada) for profoundly gifted middle and high school students; THINK (a summer institute allowing students to earn up to 6 transferable college credits); and the Educators Guild, offering free online consulting and other programming to educators.

So you may see why I was excited to speak with Ms. Adrian. I considered our interview an attempt to begin a dialogue on Dr. James R. Delisle's question: "What can we do to transform genius denied into genius fulfilled?" Dr. Delisle, first mentioned in Part One, is the author of theGifted Kids Survival Book—BTW, another good resource for teachers and parents.

The first question I asked Ms. Adrian was something I'd been wondering about and gotten various takes on for some time. "At what age should parents begin to address the needs of a gifted child?"

Jill Adrian is passionate about the work she does. She refers to her work as a privilege. You can hear this attitude in her voice.

"Well with the parents we work with," she slowly explained, "they notice that there's a difference with their child the moment the child is born. So from our perspective it's never too early."

Rather than competing with the child's needs by preassembling a path for their child, "parents can offer up opportunity for the child as he or she develops," Adrian suggests, whatever that may be—for the child in the moment— supporting them with having appropriate reading material at their level at home at all times, taking them to a museum on weekends, things like that." Good advice for any parent and child, at any level, I think. This brings to mind the whole idea of intrinsic reward—flow—

can see further ideas on flow and reward in my earlier post MUSIC ON YOUR CHILD'S MIND: Learning across Time and Flow.

Adrian diced her point down to more specifics. "Once we get them in a school setting," she added, "then it's about advocating and trying to find an educational fit for them, which can vary obviously. Acceleration is a possibility. It's also about having extended learning at home in an area of interest the child is not getting at school. We help set up a lot of families with mentors. If their child is ready, we help them find challenging summer programs. Often times, if they can't find theireducation challenging enough during the school year, summertime is when they get that."

I liked the amount and type of parental involvement that was implicit in her examples. This kind of participation is not about getting in the way. It's about walking behind the child and paying a lot of attention. It's about knowing your child and facilitating where he or she needs to go. As a big proponent of Self development, I liked what I was hearing a lot.

I asked the question many parents want to know more about. "And so what are some of the first signs of giftedness?"

"Gifted children ultimately hit developmental milestones at an early age," she said. Overall, they demonstrate a constant what intrinsic reward is; why it is important, psychologically, neuro-psychologically and neuro-physiologically; as well as paradigms for establishing and sustaining flow. Intrinsic reward—this is what it's all about, gifted or not, I thought. You need for mental stimulation. [Emphasis here is on the word constant]. They can learn at a much quicker pace; they often times can understand the larger picture earlier than their age peers, things like that. Often times they understand or ask larger life questions, they put 2 and 2 together at a much earlier age."

"You're also referring to the complexity and depth of their questioning, right?"

"Yes, the purpose of life? Is there a God? Things like that?" With gifted kids these questions seem to pop up earlier.

Again trying to think more like a father than a writer I asked, "What are some things parents can do to advocate for their child?"

Stay tuned. We will explore the answer to this question in depth throughout Part Three: What Happens Once Your Child is in the System

http://www.psychologytoday.com/blog/attention-training/201007/gifted-children-nurturing-genius-part-two-0

21

GIFTED CHILDREN: NURTURING GENIUS (PART THREE)

Carroll Doherty

Continuing my interview with Jill Adrian, Director of Family Services at the Davidson Institute, I asked, "What can be done once the gifted child is in the system, say, and headed into for 1st grade?"

"Once they [gifted children] are in the system," Adrian explained, "unfortunately in today's economy there are a lot of cuts, and the gifted programming is one of the first to go. Additionally, there are not a lot of states that have mandated gifted education and, if they do, they don't have the funds to implement them. So, unfortunately many schools don't have to do anything. We often times coach families to keep that in mind. Many schools don't have to do anything."

"So, it's about going in there and approaching things ascollaboration: asking the school, how can I help you and how can you help my child? And doing this with a little empathy about what the school system is dealing with, but ultimately, you're asking for a favor for your children at this point in time. And so presenting cost-effective options that can work for your child and your school may work best."

It's hard for some parents and educators to have to start from scratch and so wouldn't it be nice, I thought, if there were templates that interested people could use as a guide to working with school administration and local communities. I asked. "Do you have any templates of approaches that have been successful?" And I was surprised by Ms. Adrian's answer.

"Lots," she said. "There are lots of guides that are researched to help educators and families and teams. These can help the child and determine if a he or she is a candidate for acceleration. And they look at the whole child. One I have in mind is the Iowa Acceleration Scale.

Often times using this approach makes a school feel more at ease making such a drastic decision because it is often drastic for that school. Not many schools have profoundly gifted youth within their walls and so they don't necessarily know how to meet their needs and so it can be scary for them: if I accelerate this child, will I have to do it for another? What will I do if it doesn't work out? What are the social emotional ramifications? Therefore, guides like the Iowa Acceleration Scale help schools determine a good candidate."

I had to ask a darker question that many parents have to manage, "What happens when you're faced with resistance from your school? What recommendations do you have when parents hit the proverbial wall when speaking with administrators and hear things like: "Is this your first child? Everyone feels their child is gifted." Or "We take all kids' gifts into consideration." Or "Those tests don't mean anything, especially in terms of results." Or "We have a lot of smart kids attending our school. We watch them closely and try to challenge them or put them with other advanced children, especially in our English classes. We skip them ahead in Math."

I asked, "What does a parent or educator do?"

We hear that a lot unfortunately. For the families we work with it can be really frustrating when they encounter an educator who has preconceived notions of gifted students. We've written a guide book titled Advocating for Exceptionally Gifted Young People: A Guidebook that helps parents talk with their school about their child being gifted. In the end, it's about talking to them and taking baby steps. Sometimes it is about parents being willing to come in and maybe run the math circles at lunch, which will also benefit the other kids as well, not just their child. It's about brainstorming different scenarios. We've worked with many families, too, who have worked really hard trying to get something in place and it doesn't happen. And so at that point, it's about what picking your battles and determining what's most important to them [child and parent] at the time. Is it worth the effort to take the child out of school or is it more worthwhile to find an outlet for the child? We have had families who have tried to home school because their child's needs are simply not going to be met at the school."

Let's move on to the subject of home schooling. How effective is that?

"It's not for everybody. What we do here when we work with a parent is work through that issue and determine if it's the best next step. We have a lot of success stories with home schooling. We have a lot of families who have home schooled just for a couple of years and then entered the school system or went on to a private school. It doesn't have to be a permanent fix. Home school can be a temporary fix. It can sometimes relieve a little bit of the pressure."

Adrian talked a little about the Young Scholars Program, which to this parent seems significantly beneficial. "We would encourage parents of profoundly gifted students to look into our free Davidson Young Scholars Program http://www.davidsongifted.org/youngscholars/. Through this particular program, we currently serve more than 1,700 families. It's a free consulting service for families of profoundly gifted youth ages of 5-17. But they have to qualify through test scores. Once they are in the program, we work with them until they are 18. This program is open to anybody in the country. Families are assigned a family consultant who works with them one-on-one depending on what their needs are. The family consultant helps them investigate other possible schooling scenarios in their client's area which they may need to access—e.g. Saturday school and summer programs. They may even help prepare for school meetings and have even been taken into school meetings to help talk about or explain the needs of children in the Young Scholars program."

Another great resource is the book Bob and Jan Davidson wrote, Genius Denied: How to Stop Wasting Our Brightest Young Minds. The Davidson's offer a lot of helpful tips on what parents, educators, and the community can do to change their thinking about these students.

We had been speaking for quite a while and I knew there was only time left for a couple more questions—though I knew then and know even as I write these words that, for me, the conversation has really just begun.

I wanted to zero in a little more on the idea of skipping grades, especially because of the mixed responses you hear.

"From the work we've done with young scholars, it works very well for the situation. And from our perspective it is cost-effective. Believe it or not, one of the myths out there is that skipping grades is detrimental for the child's social-emotional growth; however, from our experience a lot of the behavioral problems disappear. The kids end up finding a better match with their mental age peers if they are accelerated; they're students who gravitate toward older students anyway and so a lot of those awkward behavioral problems that are in the typical age grade settings they are assigned to – they disappear or at least become less noticeable. So skipping grades ends up being a better fix—maybe not a perfect fit for social reasons—but academically, it's closer to where the child should be.

"On a personal note," I said, "I have noticed a number of very young teens entering my college classes—from as young as 15—probably for the last 10 years or so now. Interestingly, these individuals I am talking about were often some of the best students my classes."

Adrian agreed. "Community Colleges are wonderful options for these students as well. We're starting to hear more and more about dual enrollment programs and early enrollment as well. Depending on how it is set up, dual enrollment could be a subject acceleration where the child is in 3rd grade, but they go to math in a 6th grade class or they can be in middle school for most classes and they go to the high school for math and science or they can also home school and access some classes at the local school."

"Is it possible to be profoundly gifted and in the public school system? Is it possible? I asked.

We've found that the best settings for these students are those that have administrations that are open-minded and flexible; it doesn't even necessarily mean that educators have a background in teaching gifted children, it just means that they want to learn more about it and they are open to thinking outside the box and meeting these students' needs, and being unafraid to think outside the box."

Is there one last thing that you'd like to leave us as food for thought as to why it's crucial for our education systems to take the needs of the gifted seriously?

"Well this generation will be the problem-solvers of tomorrow and so fostering their growth is extremely important," Adrian said. Bob and Jan, our founders, speak about this as one of the main reasons they established the Davidson Institute. We want profoundly gifted students to reach their potential."

"Thank you for doing what you do," I said and meant it.

Adrian's voice brightened. "It's a privilege for us," she said.

Profoundly intelligent young people should not be denied what we desire for all young people. Their needs should be recognized and accommodated. Their uniqueness should be understood and nurtured. Rather than be locked into an age based curriculum, profoundly gifted young people should have the opportunity to be challenged to excel and achieve.

It seems unreasonable to expect to reap the benefits of gifted childrens' contributions if we don't nurture their minds along the way.

Yet, for as much as the world has benefited from the contributions of gifted individuals, it is disturbing to realize that the population least likely to learn and achieve its potential is the highly gifted.

It seems discriminatory to exclude anyone, regardless of his or her level of achievement—including the profoundly gifted. Unfortunately, it is easy to write them off—thinking they are getting straight A+s. They seem to be doing pretty well for themselves. What more can they possibly need?

The answer to this question is plenty.

It is my hope that this series of posts on gifted children helps answer some common questions for the parents of gifted youth, establish some camaraderie, dialogue, and strategy among us for nurturing them, and perhaps inspire our educators to seek more creative, cost-effective, and successful programming in our public and private educational systems.

http://www.psychologytoday.com/blog/attention-training/201007/gifted-children-nurturing-genius-part-three-0

22

What Does Research on Child Prodigies Tell Us About Talent Development and Expertise Acquisition?

Larisa V. Shavinina

Abstract: Research on child prodigies in general and the cognitive-developmental theory of the child prodigy phenomenon in particular shed light on the nature of talent development and expertise acquisition. According to the theory, this phenomenon is a result of an exceptionally accelerated mental development during sensitive periods that leads to the fast growth of a child's cognitive resources and their construction into specific cognitive experience. This is how human expertise is acquired. The cognitive experience is a psychological basis of extraordinary intellectually creative achievements, which expresses itself in the prodigy's unique intellectual picture of the world. The psychological nature of the prodigy phenomenon is thus formed by the sensitive periods – which explain prodigious development and talent development – and by cognitive experience, which explains prodigies' exceptional performance and achievements.

Keywords:

child prodigy phenomenon, giftedness, talent development, expertise acquisition, cognitive experience, sensitive periods

Introduction

From all possible types of gifted children, the exceptionally highly developed abilities in very young children – often called 'child prodigies' – attract constant attention of researchers and lay people. The most fascinating thing about child prodigies is that they are able to do something that is usually accomplished only by adults. However, similar talents and gifts in adults are not so impressive. This is exactly where the puzzle is hidden: in the age of child prodigies. Age means development and this is a key to the explanation of the nature of the child prodigy phenomenon.

The significance of the concept of age for explaining the prodigy phenomenon can be found in Feldman's (1986b) definition of prodigy. According to him, "a prodigy is a child, who before the age of 10, performs at a level of an adult professional in some cognitively demanding field" (p.161). Using this age boundary, Shavinina's (1999) definition of child prodigy is as follows: "a prodigy is a child who, before the age of 10, displays extraordinary intellectual-creative performance and/or achievements in any type of a real activity" (p. 26). She differentiates between general and special types of prodigies. Prodigies in art, chess and music belong to special types. Prodigies who manifest advanced level of thinking constitute the general type. At the same time, all prodigies are mental prodigies, because all of them display intellectually creative performance or achievements in various fields of human activity.

The cognitive-developmental theory of the child prodigy phenomenon states that the underlying mechanism of the prodigy phenomenon is characterized by sensitive periods. During children's individual development there are periods of high sensitivity, known as the sensitive periods, during which the cognitive and intellectual development are extremely accelerated. This is why the mental development of gifted and talented children in general – and prodigies in particular – is advanced. It leads to the rapid growth of a child's cognitive resources and their construction into a unique cognitive experience. Human expertise is acquired in this way. An individual's cognitive experience is the psychological basis of extraordinary intellectually creative achievements, which expresses itself in the prodigy's specific intellectual picture of the world. The psychological nature of the prodigy phenomenon is thus formed by the sensitive periods – which explain prodigious development and talent development in general – and by cognitive experience, which explains prodigies' exceptional performances and achievements. The same mechanism – sensitive periods-cognitive experience – is behind talent development and expertise acquisition. In other words, the child prodigy phenomenon is a particular case of talent development and expertise acquisition. Therefore, if we fully understand the nature of this phenomenon, we understand how talents develop and expertise is acquired.

In the sections that follow I will analyze the existing publications on child prodigies, present the cognitive-developmental theory of the prodigy phenomenon, and show how this theory explains talent development and expertise acquisition.

The Developmental Essence of the Child Prodigy Phenomenon: A New Approach

It is impossible to understand talent development without understanding the nature of the child prodigy phenomenon. Shavinina's research demonstrates that this phenomenon is a pure developmental phenomenon (1999, 2009). Before presenting the cognitive-developmental theory of the prodigy phenomenon, let's first of all to briefly consider the existing studies in this area. It should be noted that the purpose of my research on the child prodigy phenomenon is more to understand its inner or fundamental mechanism than various external factors or forces (for example, social or historical) that can increase the probability of the appearance of prodigies. To understand the inner/fundamental mechanism of the prodigy phenomenon means to understand how this phenomenon develops within the child. Social milieu is important, but it is only an external factor in the development of prodigies. Any external factors or forces do not provide scientific explanations of the prodigy phenomenon. Therefore, the analysis of the existing studies on child prodigies will be made according to how the real nature (i.e., inner mechanism) of the prodigy phenomenon is explained in these studies.

What Does Literature Tell Us About Child Prodigies?

Revesz's (1925) research on a seven-year-old music prodigy and Baumgarten's (1930) study of nine child prodigies were probably the first psychological studies of the prodigy phenomenon. These studies were entirely descriptive and focused mainly on the listing of children's characteristics and traits. Any field of science began from descriptive stages of its development. Nonetheless, listing the various musical, intellectual, emotional, personality, and other characteristics of prodigies constitutes the traditional trait approach in the psychology of giftedness (Shavinina, 1995), which reveals little about the essence of the prodigy phenomenon. This approach is not a promising one, because it is unknown whether the child's various traits predetermine his or her prodigious potential, or whether the latter leads to a specific reorganization of the prodigy's mind and personality that result in his or her exceptional performance and achievements.

In the late 1950s Natan Leites began his research on child prodigies in the former Soviet Union. He found that the prodigy phenomenon can be explained by high mental activity, well-functioning self-regulation, and a child's age sensitivity or developmental sensitivity. High mental activity includes the ability to pursue mental work for a long period of time, a permanent need for intellectual activity, extraordinary curiosity, and a wide range of interests (Leites, 1960, 1971, 1996). Leites's understanding of self-regulation is identical to regulatory processes in the structure of metacognition, which are responsible for planning, monitoring, and executive control (Brown, 1978, 1984; Flavell, 1976; Pressley, Borkowski,

& Schneider, 1987; Shavinina & Kholodnaya, 1996; Shore & Dover, 1987; Shore & Kanevsky, 1993; Sternberg, 1986a). High mental activity and well-functioning self-regulation can be viewed as important manifestations of the prodigy phenomenon, but not as its inner mechanism. Leites's notion of age sensitivity has a great potential to advance psychological knowledge about the nature of the prodigy phenomenon (to be analyzed below).

Co-Incidence Theory of the Child Prodigy Phenomenon

David Feldman (1986b) proposed a co-incidence theory of the prodigy phenomenon as a result of his study of six child prodigies. Co-incidence means "the melding of the many sets of forces that interact in the development and expression of human potential" (Feldman, 1986b, p.11). Among such forces, he distinguished biological qualities, individual psychological qualities, proximal context (i.e., child's external surrounding), intermediate context (i.e., family structure and its traditions), domain and the surrounding field (a key aspect of Feldman's theory), and distinct context (i.e., social-historical factors). The prodigy phenomenon is a result of a concordance of the forces of co-incidence leading to the exceptional manifestation of an individual's potential.

It looks like this theory has serious limitations. It seems that Feldman's theory can explain everything: the nature of giftedness, talent, genius, creativity, intelligence, and wisdom. Moreover, it can be applied with the same success to a wide range of brilliant manifestations of the human mind (for example, various intellectual traits and characteristics).

Feldman stated that the co-incidence theory seeks to explain all human achievement, not only the prodigy phenomenon. Nevertheless, this is not entirely correct, because the above mentioned phenomena – according to the existing research – are not the same. Intelligence, creativity, giftedness, wisdom, talent, and genius are different, at least at the level of their manifestations. Even if we suppose that differences in their natures are not particularly large, the same theoretical framework is insufficient for understanding them, because it is always possible to find something that would be different for each case, as, for example, the level of manifestations. That is, manifestations of wisdom are not identical to those of giftedness, and so on.

Therefore, Feldman's claim about the capacity of the co-incidence theory to explain all human achievement is not correct. In fact, his conclusions are correct in a slightly different sense: namely, that the forces of co-incidence are indeed important factors and probably necessary conditions for the emergence of any human achievement, including a prodigy's performance. Nonetheless, they can be viewed only as factors or conditions, not as something universal that can explain everything.

On the other hand, the following question arises: Are all of Feldman's factors sufficient for the exceptional development of human potential (as, for example, in the case of prodigies)? The answer is not particularly clear. For instance, there are many families providing good external conditions (i.e., proximal and intermediate contexts) for the development of their children. Suppose these children have the necessary individual psychological qualities (in the sense of Feldman). Finally, assume that all the social and historical factors are favorable. However, these children are not prodigies. Therefore, something else predetermines the development of prodigies.

The Socio-Cultural and Multidimensional Perspectives

The social-cultural and multidimensional perspectives can be found in the research literature about child prodigies. The main methodology of these studies is related to the application of the case-study method to famous people who were prodigies in the past. Investigations in the framework of the socio-cultural approach mainly concentrates on the study of social and cultural factors (i.e., family, school, society, and other related environments) contributing to the appearance of child prodigies (Goldsmith, 1990; Howe, 1990, 1993; Radford, 1990). In fact, these studies continue Feldman's tradition by explaining the prodigy phenomenon via his co-incidence theory or its elements.

Certainly, it is interesting to know all possible factors that facilitate the expression of the prodigy's potential, but they are no more than circumstances in which some children become outstandingly accomplished at an early age. Definitely, research on the prodigy phenomenon conducted within the framework of the socio-cultural paradigm contains helpful conclusions for nurturing and education of the gifted. However, the first and the most important question "What is the nature of the prodigy phenomenon?" – does not have answers in Goldsmith's conception or in Radford's (1990) and Howe's (1993) studies.

The multidimensional perspective refers to the analysis of the prodigy phenomenon from different intersected views (e.g., developmental, cognitive, creative, personality, and social; Bamberger, 1982, 1986; Gardner, 1982; 1993a, 1993b). In this case, the inner mechanism of the prodigy phenomenon is generally understood as a sum of various characteristics. Thus, Gardner in his theoretical explorations is a follower of Feldman's theory. In this light, he does not bring anything new to the explanation of the nature of the prodigy phenomenon. Gardner (1993a) conducted his research on the famous prodigy Picasso from interactive and developmental perspectives. Gardner's (1993a) important finding consists in the demonstration of Picasso's totally egocentric behaviour during his whole life, which can be explained by Picasso's extraordinary gifts and talents.

Picasso enjoyed the benefits and liabilities of a prodigious start. His gifts and energies meant that, with few exceptions, he was able to do whatever he wanted, whenever and wherever he wanted, throughout his life. His virtuosity was never seriously challenged, let alone vanquished... Picasso was not able to think beyond his gift. In many ways he remained childish... (Gardner, 1993a, p.184).

Therefore, Gardner pointed out the necessity of personality development for prodigies. His interesting conclusion is that there is a strong contrast between the adult creators (who must discover their own styles of creativity and the domain in which they can excel, and are formed as personalities by their family) and the child prodigy (who must construct a creative personality, having his or her domain as given by the birthright) (Gardner, 1993b).

Bamberger's (1982, 1986) research on the prodigy phenomenon is mainly carried out in the framework of a cognitive-developmental perspective. Studying musical prodigies, she found a "midlife crisis" in their development: the period of the extremely important cognitive re-organization when new forms of internal representations of musical structure appear. This is an interesting finding directly related to the main idea that an individual's unique type of representations is the essence of giftedness (Shavinina, 2008, 2009).

In general, the studies on the prodigy phenomenon within the multidimensional perspective are certainly not numerous. Nonetheless, they reveal some significant findings (e.g., "midlife crisis"), which definitely contribute to the psychological explanation of the fundamental mechanism of this phenomenon. One can predict the appearance of further investigations on child prodigies within the framework of the multidimensional approach.

To sum-up, early research on the prodigy phenomenon described various manifestations (i.e., external traits, characteristics, qualities, properties, and features) of child prodigies. Contemporary studies explore either favorable social factors, which increase the probability of the appearance of prodigies, or a combination of these factors and the numerous manifestations of child prodigies. The analysis of the existing studies on the prodigy phenomenon shows that they do not reveal its inner mechanism. It seems that sensitive periods constitute such a mechanism.

Sensitive Periods as an Inner Mechanism of Prodigious Development

As it was noticed in the introductory section, the prodigy phenomenon is first of all an age phenomenon because it is based on specific features of a child's age. This phenomenon is a result of the unique development, and, consequently, the key to its understanding should be found in the process of the individual growth of a child. Many transformations take place along the way from birth to adulthood (i.e., to age maturity). However, something unusual happens that in some cases leads to the prodigy phenomenon. What exactly? It looks like the psychological account is the following.

Unusual Development of the Gifted. Human development is not a smooth process. Rather, it has certain stages or periods. Many scientific findings, both in general and developmental psychology, testify to it (Ananiev, 1957; Case, 1984a, 1984b; Fischer & Pipp, 1984; Flavell, 1984; Piaget, 1952; Sternberg, 1990a; Vygotsky, 1956, 1972; Wallon, 1945), especially research on giftedness in the framework of the developmental approach, which reveals an uneven development of the gifted (Bamberger, 1982, 1986; Feldman, 1982, 1986a; Gruber, 1982, 1986; Shavinina, 1997; Silverman, 1993, 1994, 1997; Terrassier, 1985, 1992). In this context, the most interesting ideas can be found in the studies on the asynchronous (Silverman, 1993, this volume) and dyssynchronous (Terrassier, 1985) development of gifted children. Moreover, the Columbus group views giftedness in general as an "asynchronous development." (Silverman, 1993, p. 634). The understanding of giftedness as synonymous with asynchronous development indicates the importance of such a development for the understanding of the nature of giftedness. The Columbus group's approach to giftedness is also a strong evidence of the uneven and periodical development of prodigies. Nonetheless, this specificity of the development of the gifted and prodigies has only been described, not explained. It looks like a key to the understanding of the uneven, asynchronous, dyssynchronous, and thus unique and unusual prodigious development should be seen in a child's age sensitivity.

Age Sensitivity and the Prodigy Phenomenon. Following Leites (1971), I suggested that a child's sensitivity plays a central role in the emergence of prodigies (Shavinina, 1997). Age sensitivity is defined as a specific, heightened, and very selective responsiveness of an individual to everything what is going on around him or her (Leites, 1996; Shavinina, 1999). Indications that age sensitivity takes a certain place in the appearance of prodigies and gifted children can be found in the literature (Feldman, 1986b; Jellen & Verduin, 1986; Leites, 1960, 1971, 1996; Kholodnaya, 1993; Piechowski, 1979, 1986, 1991; Silverman, 1993, 1994, 1997; Sternberg, 1986a). Leites (1971) asserted that the child's sensitivity and sensitive periods are critical phenomena in the development of prodigies. Kholodnaya (1993) viewed prodigy phenomenon as a result of the specific development of a child during the early years. Piechowski (1991) considered sensitivity as an individual's heightened response to selective sensory or intellectual experiences. He emphasized that unusual sensitivity reveals the potential for high levels of development, especially for self-actualization and moral vigour (Piechowski, 1979, 1986). Feldman (1986b) included unusual sensitivity in his theory of prodigy phenomenon, in the "individual psychological qualities" component. Sternberg (1986a) considered "sensitivity to external feedback" as one of the metacomponents of his theory of intellectual giftedness. Sensitivity is one of the main elements in Jellen and Verduin's (1986) conception of giftedness.

Shavinina (1997) distinguishes between cognitive (i.e., sensitivity to any new information), emotional (i.e., sensitivity to one's own inner world and to the inner worlds of other people), and social kinds of sensitivity, which intersect with one another, forming mixed kinds of sensitivity. Leites (1971) pointed out many times that each child's age is characterized by one or numerous kinds of sensitivity. Vulnerability, fragility, empathy, and social responsiveness are the manifestations of sensitivity. Cognitive sensitivity is extremely important in a child's development in general and in the development of the gifted in particular. For instance, the first years of a child's life are characterized by the ease and stability of the formation of many abilities, skills, and habits (for example, linguistic abilities; Leites, 1996). Probably, because of cognitive sensitivity, children's knowledge acquisition is very quick; it may take place even from the very first experience. This is very much true in the case of prodigies (see examples below).

Sensitive Periods in Prodigy Development: The Case-Studies. An individual's sensitivity is not always the same, it changes with age. Special age periods of the child's heightened sensitivity are defined as sensitive periods2. Exceptionally favorable inner conditions and extraordinary possibilities for cognitive and intellectual development are presented during sensitive periods (Leites, 1996). The early years of language acquisition by children is a widely cited example of sensitive periods (Shavinina, 1997). Examples of sensitive periods are especially impressive in the case of prodigies.

Five-and-a-half-year-old Serge learned the alphabet when he was only two years old. At the age of three, he was able to read well and even a lot. At that time, he began to write and was able to write quite correctly. By three years of age, he had started to solve mathematical problems designed for eight-year-old children. He knew quite well the natural world of our planet (i.e., plants and animals). At five years of age, Serge saw textbooks on geography and history written for 11-year-olds. He learned all the Russian Czars and governors in chronological order, as well as the wars in which Russia participated and the stages of the French Revolution. At that point, the period of classification and systematization began, which can be considered a sensitive period. Serge drew tables on paper and put into the columns everything he knew (countries, their capitals, big cities, historical personalities, animals, plants, cars, and people's names). The child used various principles to create columns: his columns corresponded to continents, states, alphabetical or chronological order, and so on. All newly acquired information was immediately put into the tables in the corresponding columns. Very often the same information was placed in many different tables. He spent all his time classifying and systematizing almost everything. After some time, however, this period ended and a period of interest in foreign languages started, which can be considered a new sensitive period. Serge learned the Latin alphabet in two days and could read Latin, German, and English words. He asked his parents to teach him foreign languages. Individual differences in sensitivity is therefore a very real phenomenon.

Sensitive periods reveal the uniqueness of certain stages in a child's development and the tremendous potential of childhood. Sensitive periods provide temporary favourable conditions for accelerated intellectual development. Such periods occur in each child's age, even at the earliest years. For example, Skuse, Pickles, Wolke, & Reilly (1994) found that the first few postnatal months constitute a sensitive period for the relationship between growth and mental development. It looks like childhood periods prepare and temporarily conserve great internal possibilities for the development of exceptional early abilities.

Another example of a child at a sensitive period is three-and-a-half-year-old Alexei. He began to read when he was only two and can now read rather well. The child especially likes numbers and is extraordinarily good at memorizing them. He remembers the numbers of buildings, apartments, cars, and the like. Alexei's answers to the question "What time is it now?" are always correct. The parents reported that they had not taught their son to write numbers and the alphabet; the child learned the digits and letters himself, just memorizing them and writing them down. A few days ago, another manifestation of his unusual mental development appeared: adults told him any date (for example, January 19, February 5, or March 27) and

Alexei could say what day of the weak it was (Monday, Friday, etc.). He was always right.

We can see that each child is sensitive in his or her own way. Based on such examples of sensitive periods in prodigies, Leites (1971, 1996) concluded that the specificity of a child's mind depends on the age period in which mind's qualities appear. He found that in childhood years, the specific "temporary states" – sensitive periods – emerge at each age stage, which manifest significant opportunities for advanced mental development. Zaporozhets (1964) pointed out that "each period of a child's development has its own age sensitivity, and because of that learning... is more successful in the early years, than in the elder ones" (p.678).

Rosenblatt (1976) also noticed the existence of sensitive periods and emphasized that all behavioral development (both in people and animals) is divided into sensitive periods, among which there are internal relations and mutual transitions. He found that the rapidity of the appearance, effectiveness, and duration of a sensitive period depended on the specificity of the previous periods. Furthermore, Rosenblatt has shown that certain stages of development appear within a sensitive period itself. The change of sensitive periods interrupts and, at the same time, continues the course of the individual's development.

Alexander displayed his unusual abilities at a very early age. He started to read very well and to calculate before he was four years old. His interest in numbers probably indicated the fist sensitive period. The boy continually demanded that all adults around him set up simple arithmetic tasks for him; he was hungry for them. In this period, he also liked to write various numbers. The number seven (7) was especially attractive for Alexander: he wrote it everywhere in different forms and sizes painted in various colors. This "digital" period eventually came to the end.

Just over four, Alexander had a new sensitive period – the "geographical" one. He read a lot about continents, countries, cities, seas, mountains, and rivers. All his questions to adults concerned only geographical issues. He asked his parents to buy geographical books for him and looked for geographical articles in the newspapers. He watched TV programs that were about travels around the globe and weather forecasts so that he could see a map of his country. As a result, his acquired knowledge of geography was very impressive. Nonetheless, his new sensitive period did not consist only of the acquisition of new knowledge of geography. All Alexander's cognitive activity was directed to achieve one clear goal: to make a map of the world. All his time was devoted to this task. He prepared the map, conveying shapes and names of geographical objects (i.e., continents, countries, etc.) with amazing accuracy. Such an activity certainly required his artistic skills in drawing and painting, which were significantly developed during this period. In a few months, Alexander's second – "geographical" – sensitive period was almost over.

These cases of sensitive periods in prodigies demonstrate that a child's heightened level of sensitivity is extremely important for understanding prodigious development. Vygotsky (1956) acknowledged the existence of sensitive periods and asserted that:

"in these periods certain influences have big impact on all course of the individual development by provoking one or other deep changes. In other periods, the same influences can be neutral or even give opposite impact on child development. Sensitive periods coincide fully with... the optimal terms of learning" (p.278).

Daniel (an eight-year-old boy) once learned from science fiction that there might be a 10th planet in the solar system. The planet has the same size and moves along the same orbit as the earth. However, this planet is invisible from the earth because it is always behind the sun. This information immediately provoked a spark of Daniel's intellectual activity. He could not resist thinking about this planet all the time. He imagined people living on the planet and he began to invent their languages (i.e., new alphabets). The period of geographical discovery on the planet was next. The boy left the shapes of the continents on the planet the same as on the map of the Earth, but the mountains, seas, rivers, countries, and cities were reinvented. At that point, he applied all his knowledge of geography. Furthermore, Daniel realized that his mathematical skills could also be used. He began to calculate how many people would live on this planet in 10, 20, or 50 years. His initial knowledge of geometry was used to measure the territories of the continents, states, cities, and seas. All his time was devoted to this activity. Interestingly, his parents noted that never before their son had been so impressed by any reading, although he had read a lot earlier. They also pointed out that Daniel had never before been involved in such an intense mental activity.

The unusual three-week period of intensive and non-child questioning (about God, life, the universe, death, her own mortality, and similar questions) in four-and-a-half-year-old Jennie studied by Morelock and described by Silverman (1993) is another example of a prodigy's sensitive period. This period of questioning can be explained by a three-week period of heightened sensitivity to everything unknown to her (Shavinina, 1997). It should be added that the following stage in Jennie's mental development was also a clearly distinct period, with a change in her external behavior (e.g., she became quiet) and an incredible shift in her reading ability. Probably, it was her second sensitive period that explains Jennie's transformed behavior. The change of sensitive periods was very positive for her intellectual development, since Jennie reached new levels of cognition. It is not surprising that psychologists use a "cognitive leap" notion to describe her brilliant cognitive growth (Silverman, 1993).

These remarkable and numerous examples of sensitive periods in prodigies led Leites (1996) to conclude that even a child's age sensitivity itself can be considered a special kind of giftedness. Taken together, these findings demonstrate that the changes of age bring unrepeatable determinants of the individual development: sensitive periods. Sensitive periods mean a qualitatively new strengthening of the possibilities for mental growth, which appear during the early childhood years. The strengthening of such possibilities leads to the general heightening of a child's cognitive resources (as in the cases of Alexander, Alexei, Daniel, Jennie, and Serge). Therefore, the above considered findings demonstrate that sensitive periods are indeed a very real developmental phenomenon. It is not a fiction, nor a general psychological category for the combination of all the necessary conditions for the development of child prodigies4.

The Developmental Trajectory of Sensitive Periods: What Is Lost and What Is Gained? The favorable opportunities for the development of a child's mind provided by sensitive periods can be seen very clearly in prodigies as the above considered cases demonstrate. However, the sad thing is that later such favorable possibilities for individual development will weaken at a fast or slow rate (Leites, 1971). The following questions arise: if I assert that such periods should be considered as an inner mechanism of the prodigy phenomenon and of the development of the gifted, can a child be named as a prodigy or as the gifted if he or she had one or a few sensitive periods? Similarly, can sensitive periods experienced by a child be the predictors of his or her intellectually creative productivity in adulthood? Definitely, sensitive periods indicate that exceptional development can be possible. Nevertheless, it is not enough. The answer to these questions will be "yes" only if two important requirements are fulfilled in the individual development of a child. First, all developmental capacities (i.e., new abilities, habits, skills, qualities, traits, and characteristics acquired during sensitive periods; these capacities can be called developmental capacities or acquisitions because sensitive periods are a developmental phenomenon in the life of a child; a manifestation of a child's development) should be transformed into the stable individual acquisitions. Second, these acquired individual capacities should, in turn, be transformed into the unique cognitive experience of a child.

In spite of the fact that all stages of childhood can be distinguished by the heightened sensitivity of a child, sensitive periods have their own "life story." Sensitive periods emerge, exist, and even disappear during a child's development (Leites, 1971). What is important is what remains in the child at the end of sensitive period(s) when these periods are already over and favorable opportunities for mental development are getting weak either suddenly or gradually. It seems paradoxical, but it is a fact: the favorable possibilities opened up by sensitive periods allow a child to advance significantly in his or her intellectual development by acquiring something new and valuable (i.e., knowledge, skills, habits, and so on), but he or she can also lose these acquisitions when a sensitive period is over. This is a real problem of sensitive periods. Psychologists differentiate between developmental and individual aspects of sensitive periods (Leites, 1996).

If at the end of a sensitive period a child loses almost all the exceptional capacities that he or she acquired during the given period, then one can assert that these capacities were mainly a developmental phenomenon (i.e., developmental capacities). In other words, if a certain stage in the development of a child is over and all the extraordinary acquisitions accumulated during this stage via sensitive period(s) are lost. It is a key to the explanation of why so many gifted individuals who manifested exceptional abilities in their childhood become ordinary adults who do not express extraordinary talents and outstanding creativity. Gifted children lose their unusual abilities and talents in the process of their own individual development.

At the same time, sensitive periods form a foundation for the powerful individual acquisitions. If new extraordinary capacities acquired during a certain sensitive period remain in the developing child after this period, then one can assert that these capacities have been transformed into the individual acquisitions. Only in this case one can assume to a significant extent that the child can be called a prodigy or a gifted that he or she has the potential to be an intellectually creative adult.

Let's get back to the example of Alexander. When he was a five-and-a-half-year-old boy, a seven-years-old girl began to live temporarily in their family. She was admitted to school and a new educational period started for Alexander. The children did exercises together, solved mathematical problems, and learned poems by heart. Alexander started to go to kindergarten. His teacher was impressed both by Alexander's mental development and his artistic abilities in drawing and painting. The accuracy of the presentation of even the smallest details was a distinguishing characteristic of his paintings. When he was seven, Alexander successfully passed all examinations and was admitted directly from the kindergarten into the fourth-grade class of school for 11-year-old students. All of his school grades were "excellent." At that time, the third sensitive period started, which can be called an "ornithological" period.

At the age of seven, Alexander read three volumes of Brem's book for university students, entitled The Life of Animals. This was the beginning of his interest in zoology; birds were especially attractive to him. The essence of a new sensitive period consisted in his writing (or, more precisely, creating) a book about birds. Alexander wrote down the summary of the corresponding chapters of Brem's volumes and made many illustrations for them. He also used two lengthy articles about birds that he found. The scale of his work was impressive: the manuscript ran more than 300 pages with more than 100 drawings. The text was divided into chapters, and all chapters were interconnected with an internal integrity. Alexander had an extensive vocabulary. His linguistic abilities were manifested themselves in the absence of mistakes in the writing of his manuscript, which included many foreign words and biological terms. Alexander continued to read a lot; preferring scientific literature. He often used encyclopaedias and dictionaries of foreign languages.

It is interesting to mention what happened once: a psychologist, an expert on giftedness, opened the first chapter of Alexander's manuscript and began to read the description of a bird. Alexander had not looked at this chapter for a few months. Then, the psychologist asked Alexander to continue the description. The boy recalled the subsequent text by heart correctly and in detail. Note that he used other words to express the essence of the text (not the same words that he had used to write this chapter). This clearly testifies to his completely conscious work (in contrast to simple memorization).

Alexander's drawings of birds were not copies of those he had already seen; they were his drawings based on the verbal descriptions of birds. In other words, all his reading about birds was immediately transformed into drawings of birds.

Alexander's manuscript had more illustrations than three volumes of Brem. The psychologist emphasized that the boy had a strongly developed visual memory and the visual (i.e., external) descriptions of birds were the main characteristic of Alexander's "ornithology." He was not much interested in birds' instincts and their way of life; instead, he was very interested in form and size of beak, color of feather, and so forth. He constantly drew and re-drew the birds for his book. When Alexander visited the zoo or zoological museum, he also made many drawings. There were so many drawings in the manuscript of his book that the psychologist concluded that they probably are the essence of his work: the drawings were not the illustrations to the text, but rather the text was the illustration to the drawings. The order of Alexander's activity supported this conclusion: the boy first made drawings of birds, and then he wrote the text. In summer, being in a country village, Alexander was fascinated by birds and butterflies. (He had read the book Life of Insects before summer, which probably stimulated his new interest). The boy gathered a large collection of various kinds of butterflies and made numerous and accurate drawings of them. His ability to see even the small differences in the color and form of butterflies was as obvious in these drawings as in his drawings of birds. It was Alexander's fourth sensitive period. However, his previous "ornithological" sensitive period also continued.

Alexander's knowledge of birds was getting more differentiated and enriched by his personal natural observations. In summer, the boy constantly observed birds in the forest and drew pictures of them. Using his own accumulated knowledge, he began to recognize birds in nature (according to their songs, color, etc.). Every day he observed the behaviour of birds for many hours. He also found their nests and fed small birds. Remember that at that time Alexander was only a seven-year-old child.

Sensitive Periods in Prodigies: How Do They Function? The case of Alexander and the other cases presented above indicate the chain of sensitive periods in prodigies, which allows me to assume that the prodigies' sensitivity does not disappear completely. In this light, Silverman's (1993) conclusion concerning emotional sensitivity seems to be correct. She asserted that "extraordinary levels of sensitivity and compassion do not disappear with maturity. A capacity for rich, intense emotions remains in the personality throughout the lifespan" (p. 642). In my opinion, this depends on the kind of sensitivity (i.e., cognitive, emotional, or social). Perhaps emotional sensitivity, more than any other kind of sensitivity, remains in the individual during his or her life, whereas cognitive sensitivity changes periodically (but certainly it does not disappear in prodigies and the gifted). Such characteristics of the gifted as sensitivity to a new experience and openness of mind (i.e., manifestations of cognitive sensitivity) can be regarded as evidence of this tendency of cognitive sensitivity. Perhaps the availability of cognitive sensitivity throughout the lifespan determines the exceptional mental abilities of an individual.

It was concluded that if sensitivity remains in prodigies for a long time, then it is possible to assert that new capacities acquired during a certain sensitive period will also remain in prodigies for a long time (Shavinina, 1999). These capacities are fortified and developed later, and finally they are transformed into really individual acquisitions that have a potential to remain in the person throughout the lifespan. Consequently, one can predict the transition of a child prodigy into an outstanding adult who will be able to produce extraordinarily high intellectual and creative performance(s) and achievement(s).

Alexander must be mentioned briefly once again. At 14 and a half years of age, he graduated from the school with "excellent" grades. He graduated with equal success from the biological faculty of the Moscow State University and became a distinguished scientist. He participated in many expeditions, mainly to the North, related to the investigations of various birds. His adult life was characterized by the ability to work very hard, an intense interest in learning, the talent to make good drawings (especially of birds), high capacity to learn foreign languages, and an extremely clear and detailed memory. He was a great ornithologist5. Alexander's colleagues wrote:

"He was characterized by a combination of abstract thinking with deep knowledge of ecology and birds that he had learned during his numerous expeditions... He had strong will, excellent memory, and was able to work hard... He was also able to read in many European languages including Scandinavian languages; he was perfect in English. Alexander was an excellent scientist, untiring, purposeful, and persistent. He could make an instant draft of a bird or landscape... He had an unlimited ability to work... He created his own scientific school" (Leites, 1996, p.156).

What is impressive is a complete coincidence of the description of 43-year-old Alexander as a scientist by his colleagues with the description of Alexander as a prodigy done by the psychologist (Leites, 1960, 1996). The case of Alexander demonstrates that his developmental capacities (i.e., those new capacities acquired during sensitive periods in childhood) were indeed transformed into powerful individual abilities that remained throughout the lifespan. Therefore, all the above written concerning sensitive periods demonstrates that they are not a factor, condition, characteristic, feature, or trait in a child's development. They should be understood as an inner mechanism of prodigious development and the development of the gifted.

Explaining Exceptional Development. Any development leading to the significant expression of an individual's potential (in the forms of giftedness, creativity, extraordinary intelligence, or genius) and resulting in any human achievement is influenced by a number of periods of heightened sensitivity. Probably, the stages or levels of the gifted's development (Feldman, 1982, 1986a; Gruber, 1982, 1986) as well as prodigies' "mid-life" crisis (Bamberger, 1986) and "crystallizing experience" phenomenon (Walters & Gardner, 1986) correspond to certain sensitive periods (Shavinina, 1997).

Also, if we ask ourselves what is behind "asynchrony" and "dyssynchrony" mentioned above, the answer probably is "sensitive periods." It is interesting to note that there are some indications to sensitive periods in the definition of giftedness given by the Columbus group6. For example, "advanced" (that means that something might not be advanced) and "heightened" (correspondingly, something might not be heightened). Furthermore, the asynchrony term itself is also connected to the very essence of sensitive periods in the following way: asynchrony assumes the emergence and disappearance (i.e., beginning and end) of certain qualities forming to some extent a disproportionality in child development. Sensitive periods also have a beginning and end.

Understanding Prodigies' Extraordinary Performance. Sensitive periods predeter-mine prodigious development as a fundamental mechanism: that is, they greatly accelerate and, therefore, advance intellectual development of prodigies. However, do sensitive periods directly determine prodigies' incredible achievements? What permits a child prodigy to be at the level of the professional performance of an adult before the age of 10, as it was asserted in the above-mentioned definition of prodigy?

Shavinina (1999) concluded that prodigies' unique cognitive experience (i.e., experience of the cognitive interaction of an individual with the external world) is responsible for their extraordinary performances. The cognitive experience forms the cognitive basis of giftedness, which I will analyze in details below.

Paradigm Change in Addressing the Issue of the Nature of Giftedness

Before analyzing the cognitive basis, it is essential to mention the following. Kholodnaya (1993) emphasized that the main difficulty in understanding the nature of giftedness is that the external manifestations of giftedness (e.g., personality characteristics, traits, and qualities) in any real activity have been the subject of psychological research; but the psychological basis (or psychical carrier) of these manifestations has not been studied. Understanding the nature of any psychological phenomenon using only its own characteristics is unproductive. Contradictions and crises in psychology testify to it (Vekker, 1981). An entirely new research direction is needed that looks at giftedness as the unity of its two important parts: the manifestations of giftedness (i.e., traits, characteristics, qualities, properties, etc.) and the psychical carrier of these manifestations (that is, the psychological basis of giftedness).

It means that there is a need to fundamentally re-examine the question of the nature of giftedness as a psychological phenomenon. That is, psychologists should not answer the question: "What is giftedness?" by listing its various traits and characteristics (i.e., its external manifestations). Rather, they should answer the question: "What is the basis (a carrier) of those traits and characteristics associated with giftedness?" From this fundamentally changed point of view, researchers should examine the subjective experience of an individual and first of all his or her cognitive experience: the experience of the cognitive interaction of a person with the world around him or her, which is the psychological basis of giftedness or the psychological carrier of its manifestations (Shavinina & Kholodnaya, 1996).

Cognitive Basis of the Child Prodigy Phenomenon and Giftedness

If we look at the existing approaches to the understanding of the nature of giftedness, then we will see that they touch the concept of "individual subjective experience" to a certain extent. For example, Sternberg's conception of intellectual giftedness includes processes in the areas of the "internal" and "external" experience of an individual (1986).

The concept of "experience" can also be found in the creative approach. For instance, the existing definitions of creativity might be read in a slightly different way, such as creativity is the saturation of an individual's experience by a new content (Stein, 1967) or creativity is the process of the reorganization of experience (Mednick, 1962). Shavinina & Kholodnaya (1996) suggested that the cognitive experience of an individual is responsible for the ability to generate new and original ideas.

Although the number of publications is not very large yet, research into the topic of experience was begun in developmental, cognitive and expertise approaches. Walters & Gardner's (1986) investigation of the phenomenon of "crystallising experience" seems to be important. They define "crystallising experience" as remarkable and memorable unusual encounters between a developing person and a particular field of endeavour (p.307). This phenomenon manifests itself in changes in "an individual's concept of the domain, his performance in it, and his view of himself" (p.309). This reorganization of the individual experience later becomes a foundation for creative discoveries. DeGroot's

(1978) pioneering study allowed him to conclude that any creative product is not a consequence of a magical intuition, miraculous inspiration, or inborn genius. Rather, it is a result of a specific self-development of an individual, which is connected to rapid accumulation of fertile, differentiated, and useful experience in a certain field of human activity.

Gruber (1986) asserts that human extraordinariness in its important creative achievements is a consequence of "protracted and repeated encounters of the creative person with the task he or she has undertaken" (p.252). He notices that these encounters "deal rather with some ideas about the construction of social relations and of the self," than with the changes in cognition (p.254). In this period the possibility of extraordinary creative solutions depends upon surrendering himself or herself to the requirements of the task and self-mobilisation of every personal resource.

Representatives of the expertise approach, such as Horgan and Morgan (1990), have shown that one of the important results of their longitudinal study of child chess experts is that improvement in chess skill significantly correlates with experience.

Albert and Runco (1986) emphasise that non-cognitive early family experiences are involved in the achievement of eminence. They found in their longitudinal study of exceptionally gifted boys and their families that experience-selecting agents play an important role in the development of giftedness, which itself is a creative experience-producing phenomenon.

Therefore, the available research on experience in the area of giftedness (Albert, 1992; Albert & Runco, 1986; DeGroot, 1978; Gruber, 1986; Horgan & Morgan, 1990; Sternberg, 1986; Walters & Gardner, 1986) allowed Kholodnaya (1993) and Shavinina & Kholodnaya (1996) to conclude that a subjective experience of an individual plays an important role in the understanding of the nature of giftedness. Kholodnaya (1993) suggested that cognitive experience – and especially its structural organization – is a psychological basis of giftedness or a psychical carrier of all manifestations of giftedness.

Cognitive Experience and Prodigies' Unique Representations

Cognitive experience is formed by conceptual structures (i.e., conceptual thinking), knowledge base, and subjective mental space (Kholodnaya, 1993). Why do conceptual structures, knowledge base, and mental space compose cognitive experience?

The importance of conceptual structures is determined by scientific findings that indicate that conceptual thinking is the integrated cognitive formation (i.e., a form of the integrated functioning of human intelligence). The more conceptual thinking is a form of the integrated work of intelligence, the better organization of an individual's intellectual activity will be (i.e., intelligence perfectly functions; see Kholodnaya, 1983; Vekker, 1981)

The knowledge base is the second component in the structure of cognitive experience. Many psychologists stress the important role of the knowledge base in the development of intellectual giftedness (Bjorklund & Schneider, 1996; Chi & Ceci, 1987; Chi & Greeno, 1987; Chi & Koeske, 1983; Kholodnaya, 1993; Pressley, Borkowski, & Schneider, 1987; Rabinowitz & Glaser, 1985; Schneider, 1993; Shavinina & Kholodnaya, 1996; Shore & Kanevsky, 1993; Sternberg, 1985, 1990a). It was demonstrated that the quantity and quality of specialized knowledge play a critical part in highly intellectual performance and in the process of acquiring new knowledge (Bjorklund & Schneider, 1996). For example, productive problem-solving cannot occur without relevant prior knowledge (Chi & Ceci, 1987). The knowledge base can facilitate the use of particular strategies, generalize strategy use to related domains, or even diminish the need for strategy activation (Schneider, 1993). The gifted are distinguished by an adequate, well-structured, well-functioning, and elaborate knowledge base, which is easily accessible for actualization at any time (Kholodnaya, 1993; Rabinowitz & Glaser, 1985). Moreover, this rich knowledge base can sometimes compensate for overall lack of general cognitive abilities (Pressley, Borkowski, & Schneider, 1987; Schneider, 1993).

Conceptual structures and knowledge base generate subjective mental space, the third component in the structural organization of cognitive experience. Individual differences in flexibility, differentiation, integration, and hierarchy of the boundaries of the mental space influence a person's cognitive attitude to the world around and, therefore, predetermine his or her intellectual abilities.

Cognitive experience – formed by these three components – expresses itself in a specific type of the objective representations of reality (i.e., how an individual sees, understands, and interprets what is going on in the surrounding reality and in the world around him or her). It was shown that an individual's type of representations is the basic phenomenon of human intelligence (Kholodnaya, 1990, 1997). Child prodigies and the gifted see, understand, and interpret everything around them by constructing an individual intellectual picture of the world (of event, action, situation, idea, problem, and any aspects of reality) in a manner different from the rest of the people. It means that child prodigies and the gifted have a unique intellectual picture of the world; that is, a unique point of view or a unique vision. This is exactly what the essence of giftedness is all about (Shavinina, 2009).

Experimental study of the individual cognitive experience of gifted adolescents and those who were not identified as gifted found that there are some essential differences in the cognitive experience of the two groups of adolescents (Shavinina & Kholodnaya, 1996). Specifically, differences in the degree of the development of their intellectual giftedness manifest themselves in their individual representations: the representations of the world as a whole, the representations of future events, and conceptual representations. For example, gifted adolescents' specificity of the individual representations of the reality as a whole consists in the predominance of categorical (generalized) cognition. The gifted group's representations of the future are characterized by the differentiation of the vision of future events. Gifted adolescents are also distinguished by more complex and rich conceptual representations (i.e., their representations are rather unfolded and articulated phenomena). Furthermore, the correlation and factor analysis demonstrated a special character of correlations and a relative independence of the factor structural components in the cognitive sphere of the gifted group. This is the evidence of a specific integration of the cognitive experience of the gifted. To sum-up, the cognitive experience of the gifted has more categorized, integrated, differentiated and unfolded organization than the cognitive experience of those who were not identified as gifted. This specific structural organization of the cognitive experience of the gifted determines their unique intellectual picture of the world.

Taken together, these findings provide further evidence that cognitive experience is a psychological basis of giftedness, which manifests itself in the gifted's unique type of representation of everything what is going on around them. It should be noted that the mechanisms of the construction of these unique representations of the gifted play a key role in the organization of their experience. That is, those cognitive mechanisms, which are responsible for the construction of an individual's more categorical, differentiated, integrated and conceptually complex intellectual picture of the world. It is appropriate to mention here that the nature of cognitive experience (i.e., the individual differences in the extent of the development of this experience) is an important factor in the identification of gifted individuals.

The most important aspect of the uniqueness of the gifted's intellectual picture of the world is the objectivization of their cognition. It means that gifted individuals see, understand, and interpret everything in highly objective manner. The significance of the gifted in society "should be seen not only in that they solve problems well and create new knowledge, but mainly in the fact that they have the ability to create an intellectually objective picture of the world, i.e., they can see the world as it was, as it is, and as it will be in its reality" (Kholodnaya, 1990, p.128; italics added).

Explaining the Prodigy Phenomenon and the Nature of Giftedness

Taking into account the findings presented up to this point, I am now going to explain how it happens that the gifted – and in some cases even the extremely gifted: child prodigies – appear. The age or developmental foundation (i.e., exceptional opportunities for the accelerated individual development determined by age sensitivity) is a key to this explanation. It seems that in prodigies and the gifted – as a result of advanced development – the overlapping of age sensitivity occurs. In this case, sensitivity originates from different (i.e., previous, current, and subsequent) childhood periods. The description of Alexander's summer life in his childhood supports this assumption. At that time, he had at least two sensitive periods: the "bird" period and the "butterfly" period. His interest in birds can be considered a previous (his intense interest at the age of seven), current (his summertime interest in the observation of birds), and subsequent (his renewed intense interest as a variation on his previous interest makes it new) sensitive period at the same time. A new – and also current – sensitive period was the period of his interest in butterflies. One can see the coexistence of two sensitive periods. Such an overlapping of a child's sensitivity determines duplication and even multiple strengthening of the foundations for the rapid intellectual growth that finally leads to the appearance of prodigies and the gifted. Because of the overlapping of age sensitivity, a child prodigy or the gifted is always distinguished by cognitive sensitivity or any other kind of sensitivity. In this case, the probability of the transformation of all developmental acquisitions (i.e., all new capacities of a child's cognitive experience that are acquired during sensitive periods) into the stable individual abilities is getting high. In other words, the gifted and prodigies are almost always in sensitive periods that actualize their cognitive potential and accelerate their mental development. The latter implies rapid accumulation of prodigies' cognitive resources and the construction of those resources into the unusual cognitive experience that continues to enrich itself in the process of the further advanced development governed mainly by a heightened cognitive sensitivity.

Prodigies' and the gifted's cognitive experiences most likely will quickly become differentiated, integrated, and unfolded phenomena (Shavinina & Kholodnaya, 1996). Correspondingly, the character of their representations will be generalized, categorical, conceptually rich, and complex from the very early years. This allows child prodigies and the gifted to have a unique "intellectual picture of the world," which expresses itself in their exceptional performance and achievement. For example, although Alexander's "ornithological" sensitive period was very long, his cognitive experience was certainly different in each stage of childhood. For instance, his initial drawings of birds were based on verbal descriptions from books because Alexander's initial ornithological knowledge was from books, whereas his "summer" drawings were based on his personal experience of natural observations. As mentioned above, at that time his knowledge of birds reached a new level. Because of this, one can assert that Alexander had, in fact, a few "ornithological" sensitive periods. These periods can be considered as previous, current, and subsequent sensitive periods at the same time.

The proposed explanation of the nature of the prodigy phenomenon and of giftedness as whole – via the specificity of a child's age, which manifests itself in sensitive periods, and cognitive experience – is supported by the following psychological findings. For example, Silverman (1993) concluded that the heightened emotional sensitivity and responsiveness of the gifted are "directly related to their advanced cognitive development" (p. 637). The Columbus Group also pointed out that asynchronous development increases with higher intellectual capacity (Silverman, 1993). Similarly, Roedell (1984) asserted that highly gifted children will be more vulnerable with increased intellectual advancement.

Therefore, the presented theory of the child prodigy phenomenon and of giftedness states that the key to the explanation of their nature should be seen in the hidden possibilities of a child's age. The prodigy phenomenon and giftedness should be explained by their inner mechanisms. They cannot be understood in terms of various forces and factors, which are in fact social influences. According to the proposed explanation, the prodigy phenomenon and giftedness in general is a consequence of a specific development of a child. This specificity consists in the uneven, asynchronous, dyssynchronous, and, hence, unusual development, beyond which there are periods of heightened cognitive sensitivity. Sensitive periods accelerate a child's mental development through the actualization of his or her intellectual potential and the growth of the individual's cognitive resources, which leads to the appearance of a unique cognitive experience. The latter expresses itself in prodigies' and the gifted's unrepeatable intellectual picture of the world or their unique point of view and is responsible for their exceptional performance and/or achievements.

It should be emphasized that this account is true with respect to all types of giftedness or high ability. The only difference is that a specific cognitive experience, which manifests itself in unique representations, is the most important in the case of the gifted; whereas the accelerated development during early childhood is the most important in the cases of prodigies. This is why the child prodigy phenomenon is a pure developmental phenomenon. The development of all human talents follows the same developmental pattern as it was just described. Successful acquisition of human expertise is nothing else but the development of an individual's cognitive experience as presented above.

Consequently, the proposed approach to the understanding of the essence of the prodigy phenomenon and giftedness as a whole explains both the process/dynamic aspect of these phenomena (i.e., prodigious and gifted development or talent development in general) and their productive or resulted aspect (i.e., exceptional prodigies' and the gifted's achievements and performances or extraordinary acquisition of expertise).

To Sum-Up

The cognitive-developmental theory of the child prodigy phenomenon presented in this article sheds light on the nature of talent development and expertise acquisition. The theory states that the first years of a child's life are characterized by a number of sensitive periods – periods of a child's heightened and very selective responsiveness to everything what is going on around him or her. Sensitive periods accelerate the child's mental development through the actualization of his or her intellectual potential and the growth of the individual's cognitive resources. The advanced intellectual development of child prodigies during sensitive periods explains why prodigious development is the uneven, asynchronous, or dyssynchronous, and, hence, unusual development. Periods of heightened (cognitive, emotional, and social) sensitivity are beyond this specific development of all types of gifted individuals including prodigies and talented people (Shavinina, 1997, 1999).

The accelerated intellectual development of the gifted and talented leads to the appearance of their unique cognitive experience. This is exactly how expertise is acquired. The cognitive experience – which consists of conceptual structures, knowledge base, and subjective mental space – is a basis of the child prodigy phenomenon, giftedness, and talent (Kholodnaya, 1993; Shavinina & Kholodnaya, 1996). This uniqueness consists in a more complex, rich, integrated, differentiated and unfolded structural organizing of the cognitive experience of the gifted in comparison with the cognitive experience of those who were not identified as gifted (Shavinina & Kholodnaya, 1996). In other words, exceptional experts have a complex, rich, integrated, differentiated and unfolded structure of their experience. Expertise acquisition means the development of such cognitive experience.

The cognitive experience manifests itself in a specific type of mental representations (i.e., how an individual sees, understands, and interprets everything what is going on in the surrounding reality; Kholodnaya, 1993). It means that gifted and talented have a unique intellectual picture of the world (Shavinina & Kholodnaya, 1996), which is responsible for their exceptional performance and/or achievements. In other words, the gifted and talented see, understand, and interpret everything differently. This is their unique point of view or a unique vision. The unique type of representations is the essence of giftedness and talent. This is true for all categories of the gifted, including child prodigies, talented scientists of Nobel calibre, and great entrepreneurs (Shavinina, 2003, 2004, 2006a, 2006b).

Therefore, according to the cognitive-developmental theory of the child prodigy phenomenon – which is a particular case of giftedness and talent in general – this phenomenon is a result of the protracted inner process of the construction and growth of the individual's cognitive resources leading to a unique cognitive experience beyond which there are periods of heightened cognitive sensitivity. The unique cognitive experience manifests itself in prodigies' unique intellectual picture of the world. The essence of the child prodigy phenomenon, giftedness, and talent is all about a unique point of view or a unique vision of gifted and talented individuals.

One of the most important aspects of this uniqueness is their ability to see everything in a highly objective manner.

The presented theory explains the process or dynamic aspect of giftedness (i.e., talent development) and its productive or resulted aspect (i.e., the talented individuals' exceptional achievements and/or performance determined by a unique structure of their cognitive experience). Successful acquisition of human expertise is nothing but the development of an individual's unique cognitive experience.

http://www.iratde.org/issues/1-2010/tde_issue_1-2010_04_ shavinina.pdf

23

10 CHILD GENIUSES WHO GREW UP TO BE STRANGELY AVERAGE

Child prodigies have long been a subject of fascination as people want both an explanation for their special abilties and a demonstration of their talent. What is usually expected, though, is that child prodigies go on to great heights. Interestingly, many do not, going on to become fairly average adults.

Andrew Halliburton

Andrew Halliburton demonstrated great prowess and ability in math at a young age. He was routinely a few years ahead of the curve and tagged as a genius early on. The enormous amount of attention caused tremendous problems for the shy young man. He dropped out of the advanced program at his school and took a job at McDonald's. He continues to work there, but hopes to return to the university to study computer programming.

Jennifer Pike

When she was 12, Jennifer Pike received the Young Musician of the Year award. At the time, she was the youngest musician to ever receive it and she demonstrated extreme genius and prowess on her instrument. However, her exceptional abilities left her cautious. She pulled away from the scene and avoids doing anything that might harm her hands. She's terrified of burning out and does not want to risk losing her abilities through pressing too hard and going too fast.

"Gifted Children: Myths and Realities," defines the psychological processes involved with child prodigies. These children go through a great deal. Their ability to function at an adult level in certain structured domains are such that they offer a number of challenges for these children later on in life.

Jocelyn Lavin

Jocelyn Lavin studied with Anna Markland at Chetham's School of Music. While Markland went on to exceptional success, Lavin failed. Despite showing tremendous genius, she was unable to continue. She dropped out of Chetham's School of Music to study math. Unfortunately, she failed in both math and astronomy and left without a degree. Now, almost 50, she still has not received a degree, and recently resigned from her position as a math teacher.

Michael Kearney

Michael Kearney was able to get into college when he should have been in grade school. His exceptional intellect and capacity were such that he required exceptional stimulation to keep going. However, Michael Kearney did not graduate from college early. He chose instead to remain in college until the normal age of graduation. He just kept adding to his degrees. His only goal now is to go on and live a normal life, though he hasn't decided just what that is.

Kim Ung Yong

Kim Ung Yong was fluent in five different languages by the time he was three years old. He continued to gain exceptional skill in the languages as he aged. NASA invited him to study physics. He achieved his PhD by 16. However, the extreme pressure led to a severe burnout. He ended up crushed, giving up his dreams and settling for being a civil engineer and avoiding physics altogether.

Alissa Quart

When Alissa Quart was only three, she could read. She pursued modern art, writing, and a number of other subjects. However, by the time she graduated, she was exhausted. In a book that she recently released titled "Hot House Kids, The Dilemma of the Gifted Child," she discusses the feelings of failure that have followed her. She still struggles with those feelings and the pressures that she felt as a child.